LONDON AT WAR

Relics of the Home Front from the World Wars

ALAN BROOKS

Wharncliffe Books

First published in Great Britain in 2011 by
Wharncliffe Local History
an imprint of
Pen & Sword Books Ltd
47 Church Street
Barnsley
South Yorkshire
S70 2AS

ISBN 978 1 84563 139 0

A CIP catalogue record for this book is
available from the British Library

Typeset in Ehrhardt by Chic Media

Printed and bound in England
by CPI

Pen & Sword Books Ltd incorporates the imprints of
Pen & Sword Aviation, Pen & Sword Maritime,
Pen & Sword Military, Wharncliffe Local History, Pen & Sword Select,
Pen & Sword Military Classics, Leo Cooper, Remember When,
Seaforth Publishing and Frontline Publishing

For a complete list of Pen & Sword titles please contact
PEN & SWORD BOOKS LIMITED
47 Church Street, Barnsley, South Yorkshire, S70 2AS, England
E-mail: enquiries@pen-and-sword.co.uk
Website: www.pen-and-sword.co.uk

Contents

Abbreviations

AFS	Auxiliary Fire Service
ARP	Air Raid Precautions
GLC	Greater London Council
HE	High Explosive
LCC	London County Council
LCC&CA	LCC and City Area
LCDR	London Civil Defence Region
NFS	National Fire Service
RAF	Royal Air Force
US/USA	United States/United States of America
WW1	World War One/First World War
WW2	World War Two/Second World War

Picture Credits

All photographs are by the author, except 5.27.

Acknowledgements and Dedication

I have received help from a number of individuals and institutions in the research and the photography for this book. I am pleased to say that virtually without exception my enquiries were received with interest and enthusiasm. This project has occupied me, part-time, for a few years now. I can only offer my most contrite apologies to anyone who has tried to help me and whom I might have inadvertently omitted from this list. I have, however, omitted the sullen and unhelpful. They should know who they are! I wish to thank the following people and the staff of the following organisations (mainly in no particular order):

London Metropolitan Archives.
London Fire Brigade Museum.
Stephanie Maltman of Firemen Remembered.
Phil Mortimer at the London Fire Brigade Headquarters in Lambeth.
The following Local History Departments: Barnet, Camden, Hackney, Hammersmith & Fulham (especially Anne Wheeldon), Islington (especially Martin Banham), Kensington & Chelsea, Lambeth, Lewisham, Southwark, Tower Hamlets and Wandsworth.
The following public libraries: Wandsworth (especially the late and much lamented West Hill branch), Barbican and Guildhall.
The museum at The Royal London Hospital.
Peggy Crispin and Clare Troughton at Mildmay Mission Hospital.
The UK National Inventory of War Memorials (at the Imperial War Museum).
Friends of Kennington Park.
Duncan Jeffery and Nigel Harris of Westminster Abbey (for kind permission to photograph inside St Margaret's Church, Westminster).
Reverend Bertrand Olivier (for kind permission to photograph inside All Hallows by the Tower Church).
St Botolph's Aldgate Church.

Imperial War Museum (for kind permission to publish my
    photographs of the V weapons in their main gallery).
The following cemeteries: City of London, East London, Islington
    section of St Pancras & Islington, Manor Park, Old Battersea
    (Morden), New Southgate, Putney Vale and Tower Hamlets.
The Norwegian Embassy in London.
The British Postal Museum & Archive.
London Transport Museum.
David Andrews and John Dutton of Wandsworth Borough Council.
The staff on duty at the time of my visits to St Dunstan and All Saints
    Church in Stepney, the crypt of St Martin-in-the-Fields Church,
Balham Underground Station, NatWest Bank in Upper Street,
    Finsbury Leisure Centre, and The Royal Academy for allowing me
    to take photographs.
Rupert Harding and Brian Elliott of Pen and Sword Books.

But most especially…Susan Fleischer-Thompson, who accompanied
me on many trips to London's streets, churches, cemeteries, etc., and
who provided support above and beyond the call of duty throughout the
gestation of this obsession of mine.

Thank you again, everyone.

Wherever possible and appropriate, I have tried to corroborate facts,
but mistakes do occur and one's memory is not always perfect! Of
course, I take responsibility for any errors or inaccuracies that may have
made their way into this book. The only exception to this is in the
Selected Statistics (Appendix 4), where I have had to take figures,
provided by the stated sources, on faith.

Finally, I most humbly dedicate this book to the people of London
who lived through one or both of the world wars, whether they were
scarred physically or mentally, or both, or whether they were killed. I
thank any supreme being who exists that I have not had to endure what
they did.

Preface

The aim of this book is simple. It is to provide a selection or atlas of photographs of items relating to the Home Front in London during the two world wars. Most importantly, these items must be reasonably available for viewing to the general public in real life. There are (essentially) no military memorials. There is little social history – this has been done before, far better than I could hope to (see Appendix 5). The area of interest is that under the governance of the old London County Council (which ran the central part of London during the period covering WW1 and WW2), plus the City of London. This area I have designated under the abbreviation LCC&CA (LCC and City Area) for brevity in the text. However, on the odd occasion, I have chosen to include items located just outside this area. If you do not like my selection, then research and write your own book.

It is not intended to be encyclopaedic (but see below). For example, I have not included every example of surviving damage to buildings from flying debris from exploding bombs or missiles, nor of signage indicating nearby air raid shelter locations, that I have come across. I have not included photographs of every deep level shelter entrance building which still exists (although the Addendum to Chapter 4 does list their locations). I have also made editorial decisions about inclusion or exclusion of potentially relevant material. For example, there exist many plaques or signs indicating that some particular building was damaged by enemy action during WW2, but they are not all included. The chances of inclusion are greatly increased if a specific date for the relevant incident is stated, but some less specific inscriptions are included if I consider them of interest for other reasons (eg Queen's Hall at Langham Place), if a particular building was damaged on more that one occasion (eg the Innholders Hall, and St James Garlickhythe Church), or if I particularly like the wording of the inscription (eg St Lawrence Jewry Church).

There is another reason for material being omitted. I might not know it exists. London is a big place. On the assumption that this book might be considered for an updated edition in the future, please let me know (via the publishers) of any such items that you might consider worthy of inclusion, preferably giving as explicit details of the location and its description as possible – it took me about four visits to find the plaque in central Lewisham relating to the V weapon incident there (and even then it proved impossible for me to take a decent photograph of it).

I have provided a relatively detailed account of the bombing raids in WW1. This is largely because they are not widely known about, and because they gave people a taste of what they might expect in WW2. In describing the period between the wars, I have attempted to convey the build-up to a conflict that few at the time can have doubted would happen eventually. The most 'encyclopaedic' chapter is that listing the WW2 civilian war graves and memorials. Despite the efforts of the staff at the UK National Inventory of War Memorials at the Imperial War Museum, many of these were 'lost' when I started my research, and I am proud to have been able to track down several of them. I would like to think that this book might serve as a fairly accessible source book for information such as this.

Although I have stated that every item included in this book can be viewed in person, please do not expect just to turn up and expect everything to be on show. Some buildings have specific opening hours, some seem to be open or not at random, and still others may be closed without notice for private events. I think it took about five or six attempts to get me and a functioning camera into the Guards Chapel to 'capture' the memorials within, and I tried on both Sundays and weekdays. Other buildings are only open to the public on occasions or at special request. An example is Trinity House. An excellent opportunity to visit some of these buildings is afforded during the Open House weekend, held in mid-September every year, when many buildings of architectural interest in the London area are open (for free) to the public. Pre-booking is sometimes required.

Also, one or two of the items might be a tad tricky to see. The plaque to AFS personnel at Henry Cavendish Primary School in Balham can be seen from the street corner opposite, but a strong pair of binoculars is required to read the inscription. Others are difficult or impossible to photograph. For example, photography is not allowed in St Margaret's Church in Westminster, St Paul's Cathedral, or Kensington Palace Green. I am pleased to relate that I was kindly given permission to take photographs in the first of these (see Acknowledgements), but I lost my nerve with regard to the others. I have included the text of these instead. The last site is a building, which housed the King of Norway in exile (see Chapter 6), only a few yards from the Israeli Embassy in London where there is a formidable armed police guard. I saw how fierce they were with someone just trying to cycle past. DO NOT try to take photographs in this area.

A word about the location of photographed items: the address given may well not be the correct postal address (say, for a building) but generally it indicates where the particular plaque, etc is best seen or was photographed from.

A few suggestions for museums and other sites that might be considered worthy of a visit are listed in Appendix 6, along with a few which I think you might be excused for missing unless you want to visit for other reasons.

I think this is enough of explanations – read and enjoy, and if you have the opportunity, why not go out, having planned your route in advance, and see in real life some of these sights? You see almost nothing of central London on the Underground. Take the bus, or better still, cycle or walk, because then you can stop off and look at anything you want to. You would be surprised how many of the entries in this book were discovered just by walking around London, and looking.

Prologue
'Black Saturday'

Saturday 7 September 1940 had been a beautiful late summer's day. Londoners had enjoyed a fairly peaceful, warm, sunny day, and now it was late afternoon. The first anniversary of the outbreak of WW2 had passed the previous Tuesday. Londoners could almost forget there was a war on. Almost.

The first few months of the war, militarily, had been quite quiet. However, by late June 1940, Germany and its allies Russia and Italy controlled (aside from their own territories) Scandinavia, the Baltic states, Poland, Austria, Hungary, Czechoslovakia, Holland, Belgium and France. Britain had just managed in late May/early June to evacuate its forces from Dunkirk on the Channel coast, where they had been cut off by the rapid German advance. Germany could now contemplate the invasion of Britain. But before that could happen, the Luftwaffe (German air force) needed to defeat the RAF. So in the summer of 1940 the 'Battle of Britain' was fought.

The Luftwaffe sent aircraft to bomb airfields and other military targets, industrial centres and ports in Britain, while German fighter aircraft set out to destroy as many RAF aeroplanes in the skies as they could. The raids were not on a massive scale, but damage was done, and casualties both military and civilian began to climb. Yet London, the capital of Britain and its Empire, and at the time the largest port in the world as well as the largest city, was spared. But for how long?

In the late 1930s, the consensus was that Britain would end up at war with Germany again, the First World War having ended only some twenty years or so earlier. Inevitably, London would be bombed, heavily. Forecasts suggested that the civilian death toll in London from air raids could number into the hundreds of thousands. Britain, including London, had been bombed by the Germans in WW1. Well over 500 civilians in the LCC area had been killed, at a time when flying itself, let alone aerial bombardment, was in its infancy. Anyone in their late twenties or older would be able to remember the airship and aeroplane raids in WW1. They would remember the air raid warnings, blackouts, barrage balloons, searchlights, anti-aircraft fire, incendiary bombs, high explosive bombs, sheltering (in Underground stations, and elsewhere), and so on. They would remember that the Germans had intended to inflict civilian casualties in order to damage civilian morale. They would remember great loss of life when an air raid shelter received a direct hit, and when panic at a shelter resulted in many deaths by crushing in a stampede. They would remember the evil effects of poison gas used by both sides on the battlefield, and feared that it might be used by Germany in any forthcoming conflict, but this time against civilians. And no one was in any doubt that the Luftwaffe were far, far better equipped, more technologically advanced, more numerous, more fanatically led, and more experienced than their crews had been in the earlier conflict. After all, some German air force crews now had experience of combat on Franco's side in the Spanish Civil War in the late 1930s, the invasion of Poland in 1939 (which had triggered the start of WW2) and its defeat, and the invasion and defeat of Norway and then of Holland, Belgium and France earlier in 1940.

As yet, however, London had not been raided. True, there had been a few bombs dropped on the City of London in late August, and a few more bombs had been dropped, mainly in south-east London, a day or so before, but there had been nothing on the scale which had been anticipated.

And so, the population of London basked in the warm late summer weather.

At about 5pm it started.

Nearly 350 German bombers, accompanied by over 600 fighter aircraft, started their raid on the London docks, both north and south of the river.

The docks were undoubtedly an economic and strategic target. Any damage to Britain's trade was in Germany's interests, as was disruption to imports both civilian and military. They were also a spectacular target. The docks were full of flammable material of all sorts: timber, spirits, solvents, paint, sugar, flour, and so on. In the face of overwhelming odds, the defences could do little, so the German bombers discharged their loads of incendiary and HE bombs, and departed. The intensity of the raid and the nature of the target were such that massive fires were started. The emergency services, having prepared to some extent for such an eventuality but often having been derided for having had nothing to do since the outbreak of war, were stretched, and in some areas were unable to cope with the task. Many fires blazed out of control. Of course, it was not only the docks that were bombed, and burned. Residential areas, many of the occupants of which earned their living locally, lay immediately adjacent to the docks: not only warehouses, etc, were hit and destroyed or set alight, so were terraces of houses.

London had never seen such devastation in living memory.

Much of east London, north and south of the river, was in flames. At least when the raiders left, the fires could be put out...

And then darkness fell.

And the Luftwaffe came back, guided by the fires that were visible from mid-Channel, many miles away. The bombing continued, eventually subsiding as dawn approached.

Not only the raiders could see east London burning, so could the rest of London. This was it, the bombing had started. Over a thousand civilians had been killed or injured in the first 'real' raid. As Londoners looked at the bombed areas, where some fires would continue to burn for days until they could be brought under control, they could only ask themselves what was going to happen next. It was the start of the London Blitz.

Chapter 1

The Dress Rehearsal:
The First World War

On 3 August 1914, what was to be known as The Great War began. To paraphrase the historian Sir Michael Howard, Germany triggered the war by invading Belgium (a country whose neutrality was guaranteed by amongst others Britain) in order to attack France (who were not actually party to any quarrel) in order to support Austria in a conflict with Russia over Serbia. Fortunately, an explanation of all this is beyond the scope of this book. Both sides (Britain and its allies versus Germany and its allies) predicted that 'it would all be over by Christmas'. It was not. Hostilities continued for some four years and three months, resulting in the deaths of several million combatants, and injury and disability (physical and mental) to many more. For our purposes, the main theatre of war to consider was the Western Front (western, that is, in relation to Germany, Austria and Hungary, the main enemies of Britain and its allies). After a relatively short period of engagement, the Western Front settled down to a bitter entrenched conflict extending from the Channel coast along a snake-like route through Belgium and France towards neutral Switzerland. Once trench warfare had started, there were no decisive changes in the position of the front between the two sides until the final stages of the war. The casualty figures, however, grew relentlessly.

One benefit to Germany of the situation was that it now had military bases in Belgium, bases that were within flying distance of Britain, even allowing for the relatively primitive technology of the day (after all, the first aeroplane flight across the Channel had been made by Louis Bleriot as recently as July 1909). This provided an opportunity to launch raids into mainland Britain. However, the first such attacks were not from the air, they came from the sea. Coastal towns in the east of England were vulnerable to shelling from German ships – several towns in the North East were attacked on 16 December 1914. Although legitimate targets such as shipbuilders were present in the area, residential areas were hit. The impression grew that an important intention of such attacks was to frighten the civilian population, affecting their morale and willingness to continue the war.

The first air raid on mainland Britain came when an aeroplane dropped a bomb on Dover on Christmas Eve 1914. The next phase of aerial attacks came not from aeroplanes, but from German airships (of which Zeppelin, the name usually applied, actually only referred to the manufacturer of one type, albeit the one most used, of airship supported by vast balloons filled with highly explosive but lighter-than-air hydrogen gas). The first airship raid on Britain, where bombs were dropped and fatalities resulted, was over Great Yarmouth, East Anglia, on 19 January 1915.

The first air raid on London occurred after dark on 31 May 1915. It was carried out by airship, and the dubious distinction of the first area of London to be bombed (and suffer civilian fatalities) was Stoke Newington in north London. Both incendiary and HE bombs were dropped. Sources consider that the very first bomb to land on London was an incendiary on Alkham Road, N16. The building today shows no sign of this at all. Other bombs followed on the nearby area, initially in Dynevor Road. Thus the plaque commemorating the first bomb on London not only gives the wrong date, but is also in the wrong place! (1.1)

1.1 Plaque, corner of Nevill Road and Osterley Road, N16. The date should be 31 May.

The airship attacks on London in WW1 took place after dusk, the dark of night being preferred to daylight. The airships were large, slow and cumbersome, difficult to manoeuvre, highly inflammable, and in daylight would have offered an easy target to British aeroplanes and anti-aircraft guns. Navigation was a problem, especially outside the London area. The crews were often unsure about the part of the county they were flying over. Often too the main objective of the crew was survival, that is just to drop their bombs somewhere in the broad neighbourhood of their intended target, and then head back in the direction of home. They were not in the business of pinpoint bombing of strategic targets. In order to try to avoid detection, airship raids tended to be launched on moonless nights, when the airships were less conspicious. They also preferred to fly at an altitude of 8,000 feet or more to try to avoid detection by searchlights, and also anti-aircraft fire – another reason for inaccurate bombing.

The following account concentrates on those raids on the LCC&CA which resulted in civilian deaths.

The next raid of significance within the LCC&CA was on the night of 7/8 September 1915, with fatalities in south-east London (1.2). Raiders returned the following night, 8/9 September, dropping bombs across the borough of Holborn and the City of London (1.3 and 1.4). Over twenty Londoners died. It was not all

1.2. Grave/memorial in Brockley cemetery, Brockley Road, SE4, commemorating seventeen citizens of the Borough of Deptford killed from two raids nearly a year apart, September 7 1915 and 25 August 1916.

1.3. Plaque on ground in Queen's Square, WC1: 'On the night of the eighth of September 1915 a Zeppelin bomb fell and exploded on this spot although nearly one thousand people slept in the surrounding buildings no person was injured'.

1.4. Wall plaque Farringdon Road, EC1.

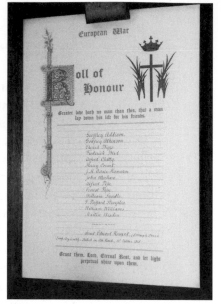

1.7. WW1 Parish Roll of Honour inside St Mary-le-Strand Church, Strand, WC2. At the bottom is the name of Boy Scout Edward Howard, who died in the raid in October 1915.

1.5. Gatehouse to St Bartholomew the Great Church, West Smithfield/Little Britain, EC1.

1.6. Plaque on chapel wall, Lincoln's Inn, WC2.

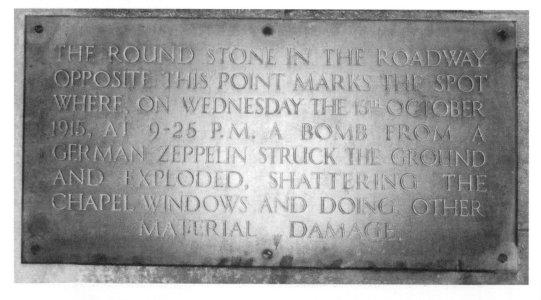

THE ROUND STONE IN THE ROADWAY OPPOSITE THIS POINT MARKS THE SPOT WHERE, ON WEDNESDAY THE 13TH OCTOBER 1915, AT 9-25 P.M. A BOMB FROM A GERMAN ZEPPELIN STRUCK THE GROUND AND EXPLODED, SHATTERING THE CHAPEL WINDOWS AND DOING OTHER MATERIAL DAMAGE.

gloom and doom that night. A bomb exploded at West Smithfield, dislodging tiling and thereby revealing the mediaeval face of the gatehouse of St Bartholomew the Great Church (1.5).

About thirty Londoners were killed in the raid on 13/14 October 1915. Again, central London was badly hit (1.6 and 1.7).

Ten months elapsed until the next raid, on 24/25 August 1916, perhaps timed to further shock civilians on the Home Front who were receiving reports continually of the massive military losses in the ongoing battle of the Somme on the Western Front. The civilian memorial in Brockley Cemetery includes this raid (1.2).

Raids continued into September and October 1916, but the British defences were starting to come to terms with the airships, two being shot down to the north of the London area during this period. Only a single further airship raid would take place over London before the end of the war. The time of the aeroplane had come. On 28 November 1916, the first daylight air raid on London took place – it was also the first aeroplane raid. No Londoners were killed.

After a limited raid in early May 1917, the next significant aeroplane raid came, in daylight, on 13 June. By the standards of the time, it was a big raid. About a dozen aircraft reached London. Bombs were dropped over a wide area in the City and adjacent boroughs, with heavy loss of civilian life (1.8). The population was outraged that London's defences were so poor as to allow such an assault. Nearly 160 died that day. The greatest shock to Londoners in the whole of this raid came from the results of a single bomb which fell on a school in Poplar, east London. Upper North Street School was hit during the morning. Eighteen children were killed.

1.8. Plaque in Postman's Park, off King Edward Street, EC1.

1.9. Gravestone, victims of the Upper North Street School bombing, East London Cemetery, Grange Road, E13.

IN MEMORY OF
18 CHILDREN
WHO WERE KILLED
~BY A BOMB~
DROPPED FROM A
GERMAN AEROPLANE
UPON THE L.C.C.
SCHOOL~UPPER
NORTH STREET~
POPLAR~ON THE
13th OF JUNE 1917.

ALFRED H.WARREN O.B.E.
MAYOR
J.BUTEUX SKEGGS.
TOWN CLERK.

1.10. Memorial, Poplar Recreation Ground, East India Dock Road, E14.

Most of them were subsequently buried in a mass grave in East London Cemetery (1.9 and 1.10).

Another relatively large raid took place on 7 July 1917, again during daylight, and again largely affecting the City and adjacent boroughs, although the death toll was smaller. Evidently, after this, the Germans decided to revert to night-time attacks. However, unlike airship crews, aeroplane crews much preferred to attack on moonlit nights, because they found it much easier to navigate their way along the Thames to central London. The bombers were smaller and flew much faster than airships and were therefore less likely to be caught by London's defences. Just as in the Blitz in WW2, Londoners came to dread the 'bombers moon'. Another parallel with the later conflict was that at about this time many decided that they preferred to shelter at night in Underground stations, and other substantial buildings, rather than take their chances in bed at home. Subsequent events caused some to change their minds again.

About two months later, on 4/5 September 1917, the next raid hit targets across south-east, central and north-west London. Again, civilian fatalities were suffered. Amongst the inanimate casualties was Cleopatra's Needle (and adjacent sphinxes, 1.11 and 1.12). Later that month, thirteen people were killed at the Bedford Hotel (1.13). The Royal Academy in Burlington House was hit in the same raid (1.14).

Another seven raids resulting in civilian fatalities occurred between late September and early December 1917, the most intense period of attacks during the entire war. Of note was that on 19/20 October. It was to be the last airship raid on London. Amongst those killed in it were a number of people in Hither Green, subsequently buried in a grave in Ladywell Cemetery, a number which was to be added to in the last air raid of WW1 five months later (1.15 and 1.16).

1.12. A plaque beneath one sphinx adjacent to Cleopatra's Needle records the event, although inaccurate in that it was the fifth aeroplane raid on London, not the first. Victoria Embankment, WC2.

THE SCARS THAT DISFIGURE THE PEDESTAL OF THE OBELISK. THE BASES OF THE SPHINXES AND THE RIGHT HAND SPHINX. WERE CAUSED BY FRAGMENTS OF A BOMB DROPPED IN THE ROADWAY CLOSE TO THIS SPOT. IN THE FIRST RAID ON LONDON BY GERMAN AEROPLANES A FEW MINUTES BEFORE MIDNIGHT ON TUESDAY 4TH SEPTEMBER 1917

1.11. Flying debris damage to Cleopatra's Needle, Victoria Embankment, WC2.

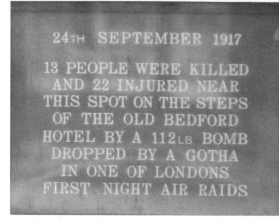

24TH SEPTEMBER 1917

13 PEOPLE WERE KILLED
AND 22 INJURED NEAR
THIS SPOT ON THE STEPS
OF THE OLD BEDFORD
HOTEL BY A 112LB BOMB
DROPPED BY A GOTHA
IN ONE OF LONDONS
FIRST NIGHT AIR RAIDS

1.13. Plaque, Bedford Hotel, Southampton Row, WC1. The Gotha was one of the types of bomber aeroplanes used by the Germans in WW1.

1.14. Plaque, with adjacent shrapnel damage, recording the bombing of the Royal Academy, Piccadilly, W1.

1.15. 'Heroes' Corner', Ladywell Cemetery, Ivy Road, SE4. It lies adjacent to and towards the lower right of the WW1 military memorial, in this picture.

1.16. The gravestone in 'Heroes' Corner', Ladywell Cemetery, Ivy Road, SE4. Sadly, it now lies flat on the ground instead of being upright, with most of the inscription (and in particular the names of those interred) totally indecipherable. At least, the top line of the inscription can still just be made out: 'In memory of those who lost their lives through enemy air raids 1917-1918'.

Another serious raid took place one week before Christmas 1917. On 18 December aircraft dropped bombs killing civilians at King's Cross, Finsbury, near Cleopatra's Needle (again), and in Bermondsey. Another bomb landed outside Stone Buildings in Lincoln's Inn, only a few yards from where a bomb dropped from an airship had landed in October 1915 (1.17). Nearly thirty Londoners died in the raid, but more than twice that number perished just over a month later on 28/29 January 1918.

This heavy raid caused casualties in several areas all around London, but there were two particularly chilling foretastes of WW2 which occurred that night. Firstly, if proof were needed that air raid

1.17. Plaque, Stone Building, Lincoln's Inn, WC2. There is surviving flying debris damage to the adjacent stonework.

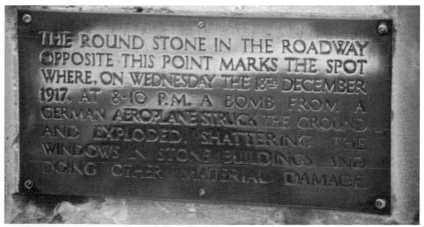

shelters were not immune to a 'lucky' or direct hit, it was provided in Covent Garden. The basement of Odhams Books in Long Acre was used as a shelter in WW1. Sadly, the building received a direct hit that evening, killing some thirty-eight people in the one incident. Amongst them was the vicar of St Paul's Church (the actor's church, just opposite Covent Garden market, 1.18). Secondly, the dreadful incident at Bethnal Green tube station in March 1943 (see Chapter 4) was foreshadowed by the deaths of some fourteen people during a stampede at the Bishopsgate Goods Station shelter the same night.

No wonder some decided, in the later conflict as well as the first, that they might as well take their chances in the comfort of their own home rather than in the not always pleasant shelters available.

The next raid with fatal results for the LCC&CA came a few weeks later, on 16 February 1918. Amongst those who died were five members of the same family when a bomb hit the East Wing of the Royal Hospital Chelsea. By one of those weird coincidences, the same building, having been rebuilt after WW1, was hit again in WW2, this time by a V2 rocket in 1945, and with further loss of life (1.19

1.18. Commemorative door, St Paul's Church, Covent Garden, WC2. The inscription reads: 'Praise God for Edward Henry Mosse rector of this church who was killed in an air raid in the early morning of the XXIX January A.D. MCMXVIII while administering to his people and for the men of this parish who died for king and country in the great war'. For those not familiar with Roman numerals, the date was 29 January 1918.

and 3.14). Another raid followed the next night. Over thirty people died in the two raids.

Some twenty more fatalities followed on 7/8 March. The last raid on London until 1940 took place on 19/20 May 1918 when over a dozen German planes reached the city. Civilians were killed in Islington, Kilburn, Bethnal Green, and south-east London. Nearly

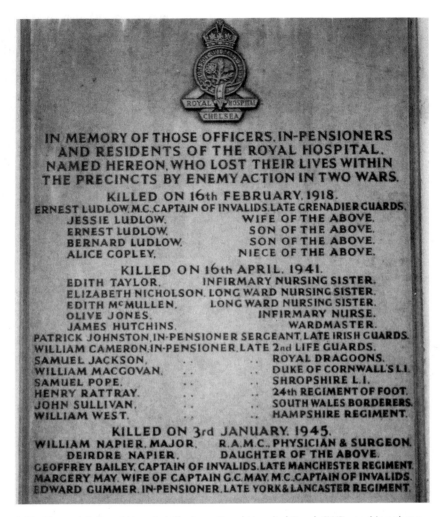

IN MEMORY OF THOSE OFFICERS, IN-PENSIONERS
AND RESIDENTS OF THE ROYAL HOSPITAL,
NAMED HEREON, WHO LOST THEIR LIVES WITHIN
THE PRECINCTS BY ENEMY ACTION IN TWO WARS.

KILLED ON 16th FEBRUARY, 1918.
ERNEST LUDLOW, M.C. CAPTAIN OF INVALIDS. LATE GRENADIER GUARDS.

JESSIE LUDLOW,	WIFE OF THE ABOVE.
ERNEST LUDLOW,	SON OF THE ABOVE.
BERNARD LUDLOW,	SON OF THE ABOVE.
ALICE COPLEY,	NIECE OF THE ABOVE.

KILLED ON 16th APRIL, 1941.

EDITH TAYLOR,	INFIRMARY NURSING SISTER.
ELIZABETH NICHOLSON,	LONG WARD NURSING SISTER.
EDITH McMULLEN,	LONG WARD NURSING SISTER.
OLIVE JONES,	INFIRMARY NURSE.
JAMES HUTCHINS.	WARDMASTER.

PATRICK JOHNSTON, IN-PENSIONER SERGEANT, LATE IRISH GUARDS.
WILLIAM CAMERON, IN-PENSIONER, LATE 2nd LIFE GUARDS.

SAMUEL JACKSON,	ROYAL DRAGOONS.
WILLIAM MACGOVAN,	DUKE OF CORNWALL'S L.I.
SAMUEL POPE.	SHROPSHIRE L.I.
HENRY RATTRAY.	24th REGIMENT OF FOOT.
JOHN SULLIVAN.	SOUTH WALES BORDERERS.
WILLIAM WEST.	HAMPSHIRE REGIMENT.

KILLED ON 3rd JANUARY, 1945.

WILLIAM NAPIER, MAJOR,	R.A.M.C. PHYSICIAN & SURGEON.
DEIRDRE NAPIER,	DAUGHTER OF THE ABOVE.

GEOFFREY BAILEY, CAPTAIN OF INVALIDS, LATE MANCHESTER REGIMENT.
MARGERY MAY, WIFE OF CAPTAIN G.C. MAY, M.C. CAPTAIN OF INVALIDS.
EDWARD GUMMER, IN-PENSIONER, LATE YORK & LANCASTER REGIMENT.

1.19. Memorial, Royal Hospital Chelsea, Royal Hospital Road, SW3, marking three incidents in the two world wars, spanning some twenty-seven years, two of them striking in the same place.

forty died, some of whom were buried in Heroes' Corner, Ladywell Cemetery (1.15 and 1.16).

Of all those killed in air raids in WW1, those from Camberwell were commemorated in a memorial in Camberwell Old Cemetery (1.20).

I for one used to think that those left at home, on the Home Front rather than the Western Front, knew little of the horrors of the

1.20. Grave/memorial in Camberwell Old Cemetery, Forest Hill Road, SE22, to twenty-two people killed in several raids in WW1. Their names are inscribed in the main panel on the front. There is a further inscription (very difficult to read now) on the base. It reads something like: 'This monument is built by public/subscription in honour of the above/citizens of Camberwell/(.?.) killed by bombs dropped/(? by) air raiders in the Great War/they died nobly + God bless them'.

1.21. Grave/memorial to the victims of the Blake's Munitions Factory fire, Hammersmith Cemetery, Margravine Road, W6. The inscription reads, 'To the memory of those war workers who died for their country in the explosion at Blake's Munition Factory November 1918'. The date is incorrect, unless it was the month of burial.

conflict in WW1. I am sure that the average Londoner could have had very little idea of the appalling conditions that the British Army in the field were facing. They had some idea of the massive loss of life taking place by reading the newspapers. But the civilian population also faced danger, and as non-combatants they did not like it. Altogether, the LCC&CA suffered twenty-four air raids in which civilians died (seven by airships and seventeen by aeroplanes), with over 500 civilians being killed. About one third of these died in a single raid, on Wednesday 13 June 1917. The conduct of war had changed irretrievably. At first, the bombs dropped on London were small affairs, although still potentially lethal where they struck. These included incendiary devices. Later in WW1, larger bombs were used, with even more devastating effects – 300kg and even 1,000kg. An example of the devastation that could be wrought by one of these large bombs came in Maida Vale on 7/8 March 1918. A big hole was blown in a terrace in Warrington Crescent, W9, and many surrounding buildings were badly damaged. Evidence of this incident survives (see 9.18).

Although not attributable to enemy action, another tragedy hit the Home Front in the last few days of WW1. On 31 October 1918, a fire broke out in Blake's Munitions Factory in Wood Lane, Hammersmith, in a hut making incendiary bombs. The thirteen workers who died, mainly women, were buried together in a mass grave (1.21). While not on the scale of the disaster at another munitions factory in London in 1917, at Silvertown, east of the LCC&CA, it represented another deadly consequence of war for the civilian population.

When the outbreak of WW2 seemed inevitable in the late 1930s, there were many people who remembered the bombing of London in WW1. They can only have anticipated what was to come with complete dread.

Intermission

The Inter-War Years

Hostilities in the Great War (most particularly between Germany and the Allies) ended at 11am on 11 November 1918 – the eleventh hour of the eleventh day of the eleventh month, as commemorated every year on Remembrance Day. Officially however the war did not end until the signing of the Treaty of Versailles on 28 June 1919 (hence the references sometimes seen to the 'war of 1914-1919').

The important question for the Allies (mainly Great Britain, France and the USA) in framing the treaty was how to ensure future peace and security in Europe. Their answer was to weaken Germany geographically, militarily and economically. Germany lost all of its colonies. Parts of Germany itself were handed over to its European neighbours. The Saar (in south-west Germany close to Luxembourg) was to be governed by the League of Nations (a kind of impotent forerunner of the United Nations) for fifteen years, after which time its population would vote on its future. Union between Germany and Austria was forbidden. The Rhineland became a buffer region between the rest of Germany to the east, and France, Luxembourg, Belgium and southern Holland to the west, to be occupied by Allied troops for up to fifteen years and then demilitarized. The German army and navy were considerably reduced in size, defensive fortifications destroyed, the manufacture of military aircraft, submarines, poison gas and tanks forbidden, and all heavy weapons surrendered or destroyed. As if this was not humiliating enough, the Allies laid the guilt for the war squarely on Germany, and demanded financial compensation from it. The financial reparations were crippling, and payments were intended to continue for decades. The German population resented these terms so profoundly that many historians regard a second war as inevitable.

The early 1920s proved to be a period of extreme turmoil for Germany, which experienced high levels of inflation and political difficulties at home and abroad. The final ingredient needed for an upsurge in right-wing extremism was added in 1929, when the US stock market collapsed. A worldwide economic slump followed, with massive unemployment. The German economy was very badly hit. Reparations payments petered out in the early 1930s.

Events conspired so that by 1933, the Nazi (National Socialist) party was democratically elected to power in Germany, with Adolf Hitler at its head. Subsequently, within a very few years, Hitler had become leader of a totalitarian Fascist regime, intent on expanding the realm of German influence, not least by unifying all German people in Europe into one nation. In this, he was helped enormously by the earnest wish of the British and French people never to be involved in a conflict like 1914-18 again, the lack of military or economic preparedness on Britain's part for another war, as well as a feeling by many in Britain that Germany had been very harshly treated at Versailles.

The Allied occupation of the Rhineland ended early, with the last troops withdrawn by the end of 1930. In 1935, Hitler renounced the disarmament clauses in the treaty, and Britain signed an agreement to allow Germany to build ships and submarines again. Saar voted to be returned to Germany. In October, Italy (under Mussolini, its Fascist dictator) invaded Ethiopia (then called Abyssinia) from neighbouring Italian Somalia, as part of his desire to expand the Italian empire. The League of Nations was unable to take effective action in response.

In March 1936, German troops reoccupied the Rhineland in contravention of Versailles. Britain and France did little. By June, Italy had triumphed in Abyssinia. In July, the Spanish Civil War started between the forces of the Fascist General Franco and those of the elected Republican government. Some tens of thousands of volunteers from many countries including Britain fought on the Republican side in the International Brigade (I.1). Franco eventually triumphed by 1939, both Germany and Italy having given him military assistance. One result was that the German air force (which

Hitler had been surreptitiously building up) obtained valuable experience for the future, such as bombing raids on the towns of Durango and Guernica in 1937. This co-operation helped relations between Germany and Italy to the extent that by late 1936, Mussolini could proclaim a Rome–Berlin 'Axis' around which the rest of Europe would revolve. Britain, by now worried by what was happening in Europe, decided that it needed to rearm in case of another war. But that would take time...

In March 1938, Nazis had also come to power in Austria, whose people then voted for union with Germany; the 'Anschluss' forbidden at Versailles. Neville Chamberlain was by now Prime Minister of Britain. Limited by the need to rearm, he was in no position to threaten military action against anyone; the only 'weapons' he could use were diplomacy and procrastination – hence the policy of appeasement of Hitler and his allies.

I.1. Memorial to the British contingent of the International Brigade in the Spanish Civil War, Jubilee Gardens, Belvedere Road, SE1.

By September 1938, problems had arisen in Czechoslovakia (as it then was), a country fashioned by the Versailles treaty from part of the Austro-Hungarian empire. A significant German minority of its population, many of whom lived in the Sudetenland (part of the west of the country), wanted union with Germany. The Czech government refused. Germany threatened war. Chamberlain and Hitler met to discuss the situation. Hitler demanded the immediate German occupation of the Sudetenland, otherwise he would invade. Britain prepared for war. The digging of trenches for people to use to shelter from air raids was begun in parks and other open spaces, other shelters were erected, the evacuation of children was planned, gas masks were issued, and ARP arrangements were tweaked. These were serious times. Chamberlain appealed to Mussolini to intervene. To everyone's relief, a meeting between Germany, France, Italy and Britain (but not Czechoslovakia) was held in Munich on 29 September. The agreement reached effectively gave in to German demands, but with the four powers supervising their implementation and guaranteeing the new Czech frontiers. The Czech government protested, but had no option other than to accede. The 'Munich Crisis' was over, with a new European war seemingly averted. Chamberlain arrived back in Britain waving the piece of paper bearing the agreement. He said that it symbolised 'peace in our time'. But by March 1939, internal problems in Czechoslovakia were severe. Faced with the prospect of civil war, the Czech government 'invited' Germany to occupy the country.

Hitler now turned his attention to Poland, which also had a large German population but whose government was determined for it not to become a German state. Britain and France guaranteed to aid Poland in the event of an unprovoked attack by Germany. The prospect of war had returned.

In April 1939, Italy occupied Albania and announced that the Balkan states were now under Italy's sphere of influence. Britain and France gave assurances to Greece and Romania much as they had to Poland. In May, Germany and Italy agreed to help each other in the event of war, and in August, Germany signed a non-aggression pact with the Soviet Union, a communist state under the leadership of Joseph Stalin, thus protecting its eastern flank.

Germany invaded Poland on 1 September. Britain issued an ultimatum, demanding the immediate withdrawal of German troops. Shortly after 11am on Sunday 3 September 1939 Britons listened on their radios to these words spoken by Neville Chamberlain:

> I have to tell you now that no such undertaking has been received, and that consequently this country is at war with Germany.

Almost immediately, Londoners heard the air-raid sirens. This time, it was a false alarm...

Chapter 2

The London Blitz . . . and After

As has been mentioned already, the term 'Battle of Britain' refers to the Luftwaffe's best attempts to take on and defeat the RAF in the summer of 1940. Part of the strategy involved German bombing of airfields, aircraft factories, defences (including radar stations), and so on, around Britain. Sometimes significant damage to residential areas occurred, with consequent civilian casualties. London, however, was not attacked, on Hitler's orders. This was to change on 24/25 August 1940, when several bombs fell on inner London, including the City (2.1).

Some claim that this was due to aircrew error, others are not so sure. In any case, Churchill, who had by now succeeded Chamberlain as British Prime Minister, ordered the bombing of Berlin in response. The physical effects on Germany were minimal, the psychological effects profound. After all, senior figures in the Nazi regime ruling Germany had promised its people that their homeland would never be bombed. The rest, as they say, is History. Germany's leaders responded in turn by threatening to destroy British cities, resulting in the subsequent raids on London, and most cities and large towns in Britain.

2.1. Inscription on building in Fore Street, EC2.

ON THIS SITE AT 12·15 A·M
ON THE 25TH AUGUST 1940
FELL THE FIRST BOMB ON
THE CITY OF LONDON IN
THE SECOND WORLD WAR

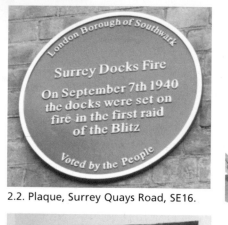

2.2. Plaque, Surrey Quays Road, SE16.

In memory of 13 members of
the Air Raid Precautions and the Fire Service
killed at Abbey Road Depot
on the 7th September 1940

Alf Bridgman - ARP Rescue Squad Leader
Fred Chilvers - ARP Rescue Squad
Ted Dunn - ARP Demolition Squad
Matthew Fenwick - ARP Warden
Fred Jones - ARP Warden
Sid Lowings - ARP Light Rescue Squad Leader
George Odell - ARP Rescue Squad
Wally Porter - ARP Rescue Squad
Frank Swift - ARP Messenger
Bill Willis - ARP Stretcher Bearer

Hugh Dicken - Auxiliary Fireman
Bill Long - Auxiliary Fireman
Wally Turley - Sub Officer West Ham Fire Brigade

At the start of World War II, part of
Abbey Road Depot was in use as an Air Raid
Precautions Cleansing and Ambulance Station.
On 7 September 1940, known as Black Saturday,
the Blitz on London began. At 7.15pm the depot
received a direct hit, thereby becoming one of
the first places in West Ham to be bombed

Lest We Forget

2.3. Plaque, Abbey Lane, E15. The site is slightly
outside the LCC&CA, but how could I omit such
a detailed, historic and poignant memorial?

2.4. Plaque, St Matthew's Church, St
Matthew's Row, E2.

Between 24 August and 6 September 1940, some bombing of London did occur, but 'Black Saturday' (see Prologue), the big raid widely regarded as the start of the London Blitz, took place on 7 September (2.2 to 2.4).

So began a bombing campaign with frightful consequences for London and its citizens. Initially, raids on London occurred both by day and by night, but soon daylight raids became unusual, the last big such raid taking place on 18 September. Londoners suffered fifty-seven consecutive nights of bombing between 7 September and 2 November, with 3 November the first raid-free night in the campaign, owing to bad weather. After this brief pause, attacks restarted. Indeed, London was the almost exclusive target of the Luftwaffe between 7 September and 13 November 1940. Just as in WW1, Londoners feared the 'bombers' moon' when a full moon helped enemy aircraft find their way to their targets. Equally, bad weather (especially over the Channel or in near-Europe) meant relative safety.

Civilian casualties were heavy, although nowhere near as bad as had been predicted before the war. The majority of Londoners chose to spurn available shelters. The emergency services had little choice. While a raid was on, they would generally be at their posts, ready to be called upon if needed. If a bombing 'incident' occurred, the police, ARP personnel, and medical and paramedical personnel generally dealt with the situation despite the continuation of the raid, as of course did firefighters. Fire brigade personnel tackling blazes during raids in the Blitz had to contend with the normal hazards of fire, including collapsing buildings, but also continuing HE and incendiary bomb drops. Many such individuals perished. Civilians bombed out of their housing might find themselves directed to a 'rest centre', which provided accommodation and facilities from whence they could be moved on in due course. Naturally, these centres were no more immune from being bombed than were any other building, and neither were conventional air-raid shelters (see Chapter 4) (2.5 to 2.25).

2.5. Memorial, Peabody Estate, John Fisher Street, E1.

Erected to the Memory of the Victims of the Air-Raid on Peabody Estate Whitechapel on the 8th September 1940

RESIDENTS

ALGERNON ARIS 30	EDITH DRAPER 73	CHARLES McCARTHY 52
SHEILA ARIS 3	ELEANOR DRAPER 44	HONORA MURPHY 78
VIOLET ARIS 34	DANIEL FOLEY 5	JOSEPH MURPHY 1
ALICE BAILEY 28	MARY FOLEY 26	FLORENCE O'BRIEN 30
JOHN BAILEY 4	JAMES FOSKETT 20	ANNIE RACKHAM 53
PHILIP BAILEY 29	ELIZA FREEBODY 65	ALFRED ROSS 46
JOHN BLACKEBY 31	MARY FREEBODY 52	SUSAN ROSS 40
GEORGE BLANKING 2	THOMAS FREEBODY 24	GEORGINA SHAW 75
MARY BLANKING 29	DOUGLAS GROOM 31	THOMAS SHAW 75
PAULINE BLANKING 8 MTH	MATILDA GROOM 32	BLANCHE SKINGSLEY 58
WILLIAM BLANKING 32	VERA GROOM 4	ELIZABETH SKINGSLEY 56
MARY BLOWER 63	ALFRED HARE 6	EMMA SKINGSLEY 60
ARTHUR BOWLER 27	HELENA JARMAN 12	FLORENCE SKINGSLEY 51
FANNY BOWLER 27	JOSEPH JARMAN 9	AUDREY STANNARD 18 MTH
FRANCES BOWLER 2	JOSEPH JARMAN 45	CATHERINE STANNARD 28
ANN BROOKS 65	SOPHIA JARMAN 47	JEAN STANNARD 2 MTH
ANN BROOKS 29	ELIZABETH KREPING 7	ELLEN SULLIVAN 55
MARY BROOKS 34	ALBERT KREEGER 18	AMELIA TARGETT 57
JULIA CLARK 63	ALBERT LIVERMORE 29	EDWARD TARGETT 19
LOUISA CLARK 24	DOROTHY LIVERMORE 31	PHYLLIS TURPIN 19
MAUD CLARK 19		LOUISA WARD 30
CHARLOTTE CRONK 75		CHARLES WHITE 31
WILLIAM CRONK 73		ELIZABETH WHITE

VISITORS

CHRISTINE BAILEY 25	66 CALDERON ROAD LEYTONSTONE	ALICE HARE 29 63 SHERIDAN STREET
JEAN BAILEY 22 MTH	66 CALDERON ROAD LEYTONSTONE	ANNIE HARE 20 63 SHERIDAN STREET
ALICE BLACKEBY 69	222 ROYAL MINT SQUARE	WILLIAM HARE 24 63 SHERIDAN STREET
JOHN BLACKEBY 67	222 ROYAL MINT SQUARE	ELIZABETH KENTER 48 42 HALF MOON PASSAGE
ALICE CLEWLEY 14	19 AYLWARD STREET	ELLEN WHITE 18 28 CUTTLE CLOSE
VERNON ELY 26	28 EASTMINSTER	WILLIAM WRIGHT 69 63 SHERIDAN STREET

THESE TREES WERE PROVIDED BY
LOCAL RESIDENTS AND THE CHILDREN
OF HALLSVILLE COUNTY PRIMARY SCHOOLS
TO PERPETUATE THE MEMORY OF THOSE
WHO LOST THEIR LIVES
IN A BOMBING RAID ON THIS SITE
ON SEPTEMBER 10TH 1940

2.6. Plaque, Hallsville Primary School, Radland Road, E16. The school, which lies just outside the LCC& CA, was being used as a rest centre. It is not known for certain how many were killed when it was hit in a subsequent raid (the council's official figure was seventy-three, but it may have been as many as 400. It may represent the highest death toll from a single bomb in the whole of Britain). The story goes that many of these deaths were avoidable – it is said that a coach sent to transfer shelterers elsewhere failed to do so because it went to Camden Town, instead of Canning Town…

In memory of the people
of Camberwell who died
or suffered in War

This memorial stands above the Air Raid
Shelter where a wedding party lost their lives
on the afternoon of 17 September 1940.

Sidney and Patricia Wright had just married
and were celebrating in the nearby 'Father
Redcap' Public House with family and friends.

During an air raid, they sought refuge in the
shelter which was directly hit by a bomb. All
members of the Wright family and four other
people were killed.

May they, and all victims
of War, rest in peace

2.7. Plaque commemorating the awful story of 17 September 1940 in Camberwell (see also 2.8). Camberwell Green, SE5.

2.8. Second plaque, accompanying that shown in 2.7. Camberwell Green, SE5. Both plaques lie in a small area in the Green representing the site of the air-raid shelter.

Bodies recovered from the Air Raid Shelter
on 18 September 1940:

Wright family
Bride and Groom - Patricia and Sidney (aged 21)
Sidney's parents - Elizabeth and Sidney (aged 48)
Sidney's sisters - Dorothy (aged 19) Mary (aged 18)
Elsie (aged 13) Joyce (aged 10) and June (aged 8)

Nora Flaherty (aged 19) Lear Nadel (aged 58)
Emma Ross (aged 48) and her son Stanley Ross (aged 14)

2.9. Inscription on John Lewis department store, Holles Street, W1. The original building was severely damaged on 18 September 1940.

2.10. Plaque outside St Luke's Primary School, Saunders Ness Road, E14. It reads: 'In memory of Auxiliary Firewomen Joan Bartlett and Violet Pengelly who died on this site as a result of enemy action on the night of 18th/19th September 1940 when the school then in use as Sub Fire Station 35U received a direct hit from a high-explosive bomb. In memory also of 24 members of the ARP/Civil Defence Services who died with them – (names) Auxiliary Ambulance Drivers, (names) Stretcher Bearers, (names) Doctors/Nurses, (name) Warden'.

THIS TABLET WAS REMOVED

FROM THE BRANCH WHICH

STOOD ON THIS SITE UNTIL

THE PREMISES WERE DESTROYED

BY ENEMY ACTION ON THE

NIGHT OF 22ND SEPTEMBER 1940

2.11. Plaque, Highbury and Islington branch, NatWest Bank, Upper Street, N1.

2.12. St Margaret's Church, St Margaret Street, SW1, was hit by an oil bomb on 25 September 1940. There is residual charring on the end of pew 38 from the resulting fire. The pews in front of this were more badly damaged, and have been replaced with unadorned woodwork (see also 2.13).

2.13 The James Palmer memorial on the wall adjacent to the pews shown in 2.12 was damaged in the same raid, and together with the panel beneath, remains blackened along its left side as a result. A small photograph with inscription mounted on the wall to its lower right explains what happened.

2.14. Plaque, southbound platform Bounds Green Underground station, Bounds Green Road, N11.

2.15. Plaque, Jamaica Road, SE16.

THE NORTHWEST CORNER OF THIS BUILDING WAS DESTROYED BY BOMBS ON THE 14TH OCTOBER 1940: AND REBUILT IN 1947.

THIS STONE AND THE GARGOYLE ABOVE WERE TAKEN FROM A PART OF THE HOUSES OF PARLIAMENT ALSO DAMAGED IN THE AIR RAIDS

In memory of the 64 people killed at this station by a wartime bomb 14th October 1940

2.16. Plaque in entrance hall Balham Underground Station, Balham High Road, SW12.

2.17. Plaque inside St James's Church, Piccadilly, SW1 (see also 2.18).

2.18. Plaque outside St James's Church, Piccadilly, SW1 (see also 2.17).

2.19. Many shelterers in the basement of Alice Owens School were killed by a direct hit on the school on 14 October 1940. This memorial is sited outside the Centre for Applied Sciences, City and Islington College, Goswell Road, EC1.

2.20. Plaque inside entrance, Morley College, Westminster Bridge Road, SE1. The building is only a short distance from where the shelter in Kennington Park was hit less than thirty minutes later on the same evening (2.21). The plaque records '...the destruction by enemy action of the main building of Morley College on the evening of October 15th 1940 with the loss of fifty seven lives while it was in use as a Rest Centre...'

2.22. Plaque, Druid Street, SE1.

2.21. Memorial to the victims of the bombing of the trench shelter in Kennington Park, Kennington Park Road, SE11, 15 October 1940. Photograph taken on the day of its unveiling. Officially, over fifty died. Local people estimate over twice this many were killed. There is speculation that the remaining bodies were left because the local rescue services were overstretched in the area at the time (see 2.20).

The main bombs dropped on London during the war were either HE or incendiary in type. The commonest HE bombs used, especially in the earlier part of the Blitz, were 50 and 250kg bombs, but larger bombs were also used, with the very largest weighing in at 1,800, 2,000 and 2,500kg. As a general rule, about half the weight of an HE bomb consisted of the explosive, so the destructive power of the largest HE bombs was roughly equivalent to that of a V weapon (see Chapter 3). So-called parachute mines were indeed naval-style mines, suspended by a parachute so their descent was silent and not in the least accurate. The vast majority of incendiary bombs were small, about 1kg in weight, but as we will see, capable of causing considerable damage. 'Oil bombs' were effectively HE incendiary bombs. As far as I am aware, the most comprehensive display of the bombs used against London is on show at the Imperial War Museum, although others may be seen in The Museum of Docklands and the museum of the Royal Hospital Chelsea, for example (see Appendix 6 for addresses).

Although Londoners enjoyed something of a respite at this point, no longer suffering raids every night, the bombers still came back at intervals. From mid-November 1940 to late January 1941, raids against London were fewer in number, but several large and a number of smaller raids occurred (2.26 to 2.30).

2.23. Memorial inside St Peter's Church, Liverpool Grove, SE17. The church's crypt was used as an air-raid shelter. During the raid on 29 October 1940, an HE bomb penetrated the roof and floor of the church, finally exploding once it had reached the crypt. At least sixty-five people were killed.

2.24. Gravestone, Wandsworth Cemetery, Magdalen Road, SW18.

2.25. Plaque, Henry Cavendish Primary School, Hydethorpe Road, SW12. It reads, 'In memory of thirteen members of the London Auxiliary Fire Service killed by enemy action while on duty on this site, then in use as Sub Fire Station 86W, on the night of 6th November 1940'. A list of names is then inscribed.

The most famous raid in this phase was called by some the 'Second Great Fire of London'. On the night of 29/30 December 1940, a time when much of the City of London was empty of people (and firewatchers) because of the Christmas and New Year period, the Luftwaffe launched an intense raid against the City. While many HE bombs were dropped, a major weapon in this raid was the incendiary bomb. These were small but had significant penetrating power. If they landed on the roof of a building, be it a warehouse, residential block, church, cathedral, or anything (or indeed anywhere) else, a fire would be started. By this stage of the war, most people knew how to deal with such bombs if they were spotted. But if a bomb penetrated a roof into the roof space or loft, or the interior of a building left unoccupied for the holiday season, a brisk fire was

2.26. Plaque outside Fire Station, West Hill, SW18.

2.27. Gravestones marking those killed at Wandsworth Fire Station (2.26). Streatham Cemetery, Garratt Lane, SW17.

2.28. Gravestone of more AFS casualties of the Blitz, this time at Gainsborough Road School, West Ham, on 8 December 1940. East London Cemetery, Grange Road, E13. There is a Firemen Remembered plaque on the school building also (not illustrated).

2.29. Plaque outside All Soul's Church, Langham Place, W1.

likely to break out, which if unchecked would destroy the building. So it was that, despite the best efforts of the fire services, much of the City of London was devastated by fire that night, and surrounding areas were also hit (2.31 to 2.35).

Between mid-January and early March 1941, London and the rest of Britain experienced another relative lull, with only a few comparatively light raids. Sadly, this did not mean that Londoners were safe (2.36).

London received a relatively small number of raids between 8 March and 10/11 May, but these included some of the biggest raids Londoners experienced during the entire Blitz. Even the smaller

2.30. Plaque to rear of Twining's, Fleet Street, EC4.

2.31. Plaque on building in Tooley Street, SE1.

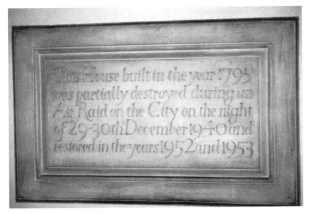

2.32. Plaque inside Trinity House, Trinity Square, EC3.

2.33. Memorial inside All Hallows by the Tower Church, Byward Street, EC3. Like many other buildings, several churches were damaged on several dates during WW2, and this one was amongst that number. Its main wounds were however suffered on 29/30 December 1940. The eastern wall of the church was rebuilt in much the same manner as the tower of Bow Church (see 5.28). On the outside of this wall is a simple plaque which summarizes, in Latin, the history of the church.

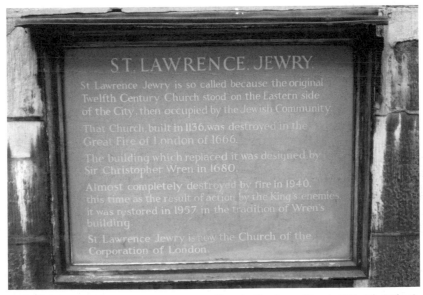

2.34. Plaque outside St Lawrence Jewry Church, Gresham Street, EC2. 'The King's enemies' almost destroyed this church - on the same night as several others (see 2.33 and 2.35).

CHRISTCHURCH - GREYFRIARS
THIS WREN CHURCH WAS DESTROYED -
BY FIRE-BOMBS IN DECEMBER 1940.
UNDER THE PASTORAL REORGANISATION
MEASURE OF 1949, THE PARISH OF
CHRISTCHURCH WAS UNITED WITH
ST SEPULCHRE-WITHOUT-NEWGATE
HOLBORN VIADUCT E.C.1

2.35. Plaque near ruins of Christchurch Greyfriars, Newgate Street, EC1, another victim of 'The Second Great Fire of London'.

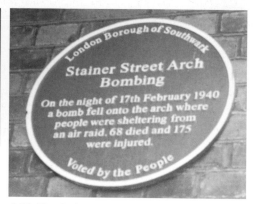

London Borough of Southwark

Stainer Street Arch Bombing

On the night of 17th February 1940 a bomb fell onto the arch where people were sheltering from an air raid. 68 died and 175 were injured.

Voted by the People

2.36. The Stainer Street incident near London Bridge Station. The date should of course read '1941'. Stainer Street, SE1.

raids could be deadly (2.37 and 2.38). There were three big raids in April and May 1941: 16/17 April ('The Wednesday'), 19/20 April ('The Saturday', twenty April being Hitler's 52nd birthday), and 10/11 May ('The last and worst raid of the London Blitz') (2.39 to 2.58). By the morning of 11 May, London had been damaged widely, with much loss of life, disruption to utilities and public transport, and damage to many famous and historical buildings. It had indeed been a bad raid. It is widely regarded as the last raid of the London Blitz, although it was not the last air raid by aircraft by any means (and of course the V1 and V2 raids were to follow three years later), but it serves as a stark bookend, marking the end of a particularly gruelling phase of the war.

Between 7 September 1940 and 11 May 1941, London and its population had been battered. How long could they stand this sort of punishment? Fortunately, we will never know. Raids became very few and far between, from mid-May 1941 to the end of 1942. These include 27/28 July 1941: several graves bearing the date lie in Tower Hamlets Cemetery (2.59). Superficially, the reasons for the pause are easy to see: the Luftwaffe was needed elsewhere. Despite what had happened, the British public were not clamouring for a negotiated peace (something which would have delighted Germans), and Germany decided against an invasion of Britain (protected as it was by the RAF and Royal Navy). Germany had also just conquered Greece and Yugoslavia, driving out Allied forces to Crete, which it

In Memory of
Auxiliary Fireman Albert Edward Arber
who served under Station 32 Bow and
who died as a result of enemy action
buried by falling masonry at the junction
of St. Stephens Road and Athelstane Grove
on the night of 19th/20th March 1941
when a high explosive bomb demolished
two houses near this site.

*This plaque remembers also
Auxiliary Fireman David William Carson
(1912 - 2006)
who served on Bow Fire Station's ground
in World War II and through whom
this memorial was made possible.*

2.37. Plaque in Athelstone Grove, E3. Somewhat confusingly, many East Enders referred to 19/20 March 1941 as 'The Wednesday' (because the East End was very badly affected by that raid), whereas most other Londoners used the term to refer to the raid on the night of 16/17 April 1941.

2.38. Plaque on building in Dod Street, E14.

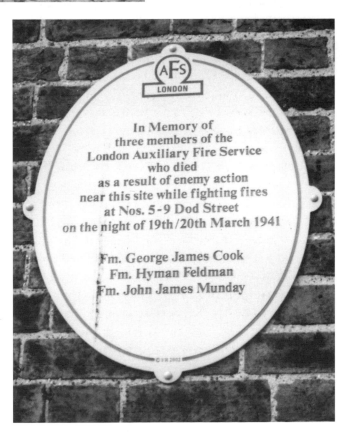

In Memory of
three members of the
London Auxiliary Fire Service
who died
as a result of enemy action
near this site while fighting fires
at Nos. 5 - 9 Dod Street
on the night of 19th/20th March 1941

Fm. George James Cook
Fm. Hyman Feldman
Fm. John James Munday

proceeded to attack on 20 May. Despite declining to send an invading force against Britain, Germany did decide to attack the Soviet Union, its former ally and a huge opponent both in terms of population and area, on 22 June 1941. The higher echelons of the Soviet military had largely been removed in Stalin's purges, and so its military capacity was now weakened and theoretically beatable. One wonders, however, how Germany could possibly have occupied such a vast territory, even if it had won, in addition to its military occupation of the bulk of mainland Europe. But take on the Soviet Union, Germany did. This time, the rest was Geography, Meteorology, and Sushi.

As 1941 wore on, the German advance into Russia faltered. The front line forces needed food, water, munitions, fuel, and maintenance of their equipment, but the supply lines were extremely long. The weather worsened. Soviet resolve stiffened, and a major confrontation took place at Stalingrad. It had all been going so well, until now. And just when you think that things could not get any worse, your inscrutable Japanese allies decide they are going to bomb a naval base in Pearl Harbour in Hawaii. This just happened to be the base of the Pacific Fleet of the USA, the most powerful nation on earth who, until now, had been determined to sit on their hands in

Chelsea Hospital, Royal Hospital Road, SW3, hit during the raid on the 'Wednesday'.

THIS CHURCH RECORDS OF WHICH DATE FROM
THE THIRTEENTH CENTURY WAS RECONSECRATED BY
HENRY LORD BISHOP OF LONDON IN THE PRESENCE OF
HER MAJESTY
QUEEN ELIZABETH THE QUEEN MOTHER
ON THE 13TH MAY 1958
THE PRESENT BUILDING REPLACES THAT BOMBED ON THE
NIGHT OF THE 16TH APRIL 1941 WHEN FIVE FIRE WATCHERS
WERE KILLED · HENRY FRANKLAND · YVONNE GREEN
MICHAEL HODGE · SIDNEY SIMS · FREDERICK WINTER
IN WHOSE MEMORY THIS STONE IS ERECTED
VICAR · C E LEIGHTON THOMSON
CHURCHWARDENS · JOHN W DURNFORD · ARTHUR P H STRIDE
ARCHITECT · WALTER H GODFREY

2.41. Plaque inside Chelsea Old Church, Old Church Street, SW3 (see also 2.42 and 2.43).

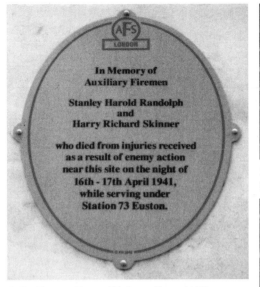

2.40. Plaque, Upper Woburn Place, WC1.

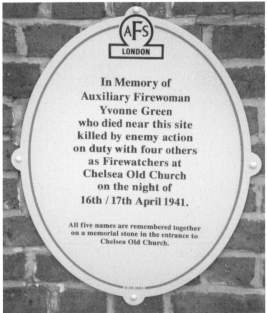

In Memory of
Auxiliary Firewoman
Yvonne Green
who died near this site
killed by enemy action
on duty with four others
as Firewatchers at
Chelsea Old Church
on the night of
16th / 17th April 1941.

All five names are remembered together
on a memorial stone in the entrance to
Chelsea Old Church.

2.44. Plaque outside the City Temple, Holborn Viaduct, EC1.

2.43. Plaque, Chelsea Embankment, SW3 (see also 2.41 and 2.42).

2.42. Plaque, Old Church Street, SW3 (see also 2.41 and 2.43)

2.45. Memorial in garden of Christ Church, Blackfriars Road, SE1 (see also 2.46).

2.46. Another view of the memorial, and the cross, at Christ Church (see also 2.45).

2.47. Plaque outside Chelsea Fire Station, King's Road, SW3.

2.48. Plaque outside the Young Vic theatre in The Cut, SE1. There is also a handwritten list of the victims on the wall inside the theatre, near the box office.

2.49. Gravestone for more AFS personnel, this time killed on 'The Saturday'. East London Cemetery, Grange Road, E13.

In Loving Memory of
My Dear Husband
CHARLES EDWARD
RAPLEY (A.R.P)
KILLED BY ENEMY ACTION
19TH APRIL 1941.
AGED 40 YEARS.
DEATH DOES NOT BREAK

2.50. Gravestone, Lambeth Cemetery, Blackshaw Road, SW17, reminding us that ARP workers were also involved in a dangerous task during raids.

In memory of the 13 London firemen
and women and 21 Beckenham
firemen killed on the night
of 19th April 1941 when a bomb
destroyed the old school being
used as a sub-fire station.

This is the largest single loss of Fire
Brigade personnel in English history.

Details of this tragic incident were recorded in
the wartime diaries of Mr W. Somerville,
an off duty member of the Homerton crew.

It is to him and the many thousands of men
and women that made up the A.F.S & N.F.S
1939 - 1945 that this plaque is also dedicated.

2.51. Plaque on wall of school in St Leonard's Street, E3. The inscription says it all (see also 2.52).

IN FREEDOMS CAUSE
SACRED TO THE MEMORY OF
TWENTY ONE GALLANT MEMBERS OF
THE BECKENHAM AUXILIARY FIRE SERVICE
KILLED BY ENEMY ACTION WHILST ON DUTY 19-20 APRIL 1941.

IF W.J.WOODLAND	IF L.ROOTS	IF M.C.PARFETT	IF E.W.VICK
F.J.ENDEAN	R.M.BAILEY	R.C.AITCHISON	K.J.BOWLES
A.V.KITE	A.C.BARBER	H.J.CARDEN	R.J.DEANS
A.E.MINTER	G.J.J.HALL	INTERRED AT WEST WICKHAM	C.FARLEY
A.G.WOTTON	F.G.PARCELL	E.R.BEADLE	L.T.HEALEY
	W.G.PLANT	H.R.MOUNTJOY	

AT THE GOING DOWN OF THE SUN AND IN THE MORNING WE WILL REMEMBER THEM.

2.52. Grave of the firemen from Beckenham killed on 19/20 April 1941 (2.51). Beckenham Cemetery, Elmers End Road, Beckenham.

2.53. Plaque, Brewhouse Street, SW15.

This plaque has been placed here in memory of the 45 people who lost their lives in the Castle public house on the 19th April 1941 during a World War II bomb attack

2.54. Plaque set into the ground, Lamb Building, Temple, EC4.

LAMB BUILDING STOOD HERE BUILT IN 1667 DESTROYED BY ENEMY ACTION 11TH. MAY 1941

2.55. St Botolph's Church, Aldgate High Street, EC3, had a lucky escape in the great May 1941 raid. This floor plaque marks the site where a bomb landed, having pierced the roof. It did not explode.

In Memory of
Auxiliary Fireman
Abraham Lewis

who died from injuries received
when called to incendiary fires
at Trinity House
on the night of
10th/11th May 1941

2.56. Plaque inside Trinity House, Trinity Square, EC3.

2.57. Plaque in Langham Place, W1, marking the destruction of the Queen's Hall which occurred on 10/11 May 1941.

2.58. Plaque on building in Blackfriars Road, SE1.

2.59. Two of the graves in Tower Hamlets Cemetery, Southern Grove, E3, where victims of the 27/28 July 1941 raid were buried.

2.60. Grave in Hither Green Cemetery, Verdant Lane, SE6. 'Sacred to the memory of 38 children and 6 teachers who were killed when Sandhurst Road School was bombed by a lone German aeroplane on Wednesday 20th January 1943'. There are memorials at the school in Ardgowan Road/Sandhurst Road, SE6, but these are not readily visible to the public. My enquiry to them about this received no reply.

this conflict and avoid getting involved. Japan attacked on 7 December 1941. The next day, the USA declared war on Japan, and Germany declared war on the USA.

With all these other diversions, as well as a desert campaign in North Africa against the British, it is hardly surprising that the next two and a half years or so saw a dramatic fall in the number of air raids against mainland Britain. The odd surprise attack, often by a small number of aircraft, did still take place, sometimes with tragic consequences.

At lunchtime on Wednesday 20 January 1943, during a hit-and-run daylight raid, Sandhurst Road School in Catford was bombed. Some thirty-eight children and six teachers were killed (2.60).

Less certain was the number who perished when bombs hit the Cinderella Dancing Club in Putney on the evening of Sunday 7 November 1943. The place was packed with youngsters enjoying themselves. It was not known how many people were present at the time, and many were literally blown to pieces (2.61).

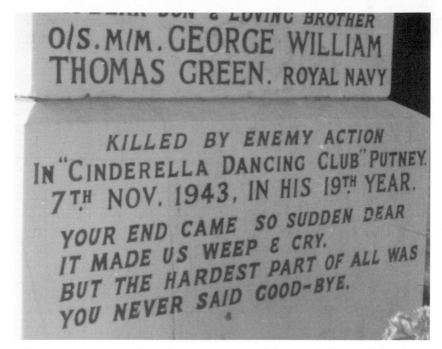

O/S. M/M. GEORGE WILLIAM THOMAS GREEN. ROYAL NAVY

KILLED BY ENEMY ACTION IN "CINDERELLA DANCING CLUB" PUTNEY. 7TH NOV. 1943, IN HIS 19TH YEAR.

YOUR END CAME SO SUDDEN DEAR IT MADE US WEEP & CRY. BUT THE HARDEST PART OF ALL WAS YOU NEVER SAID GOOD-BYE.

2.61. Gravestone, Wandsworth Cemetery, Magdalen Road, SW18. The club, in Putney High Street SW15, was busy with youngsters on a Sunday evening in autumn when it was hit. The exact death toll is not known – being a place of entertainment, only the identities of the staff and members of the band were known. Many bodies were 'unidentifiable'.

2.62. Plaque in Gwendwr Garden, Gunterstone Road, W14.

METROPOLITAN BOROUGH OF FULHAM

GWENDWR GARDEN

THE LAND FORMING THE SITE OF THIS GARDEN WAS PRESENTED TO THE METROPOLITAN BOROUGH OF FULHAM BY ROBERT GEOFFREY GUNTER ESQ., TO BE LAID OUT BY THE BOROUGH COUNCIL AND USED AS A MEMORIAL GARDEN TO COMMEMORATE THE EXTENSIVE DAMAGE SUFFERED IN THE WEST KENSINGTON AREA OF THE BOROUGH DURING ENEMY AIR ACTION PARTICULARLY ON THE NIGHT OF 20TH FEBRUARY. 1944.

THIS GARDEN WAS FORMALLY OPENED BY HIS WORSHIP THE MAYOR OF FULHAM COUNCILLOR ALAN J. JIGGINS. ON SATURDAY. 23RD JULY. 1949.

E. R. KNIGHT. M.ENG., M.I.MIN. E., ETC.
BOROUGH SURVEYOR

CYRIL F. THATCHER. LL.B.
TOWN CLERK

2.63. Plaque at Dovehouse Green, King's Road, SW3, just beneath a plaque to the civilian dead of the Metropolitan Borough of Chelsea (8.12), commemorating the gallantry of Anthony Smith and Albert Littlejohn. One of the Guinness Trust buildings on the Kings Road, SW10, was hit during the Baby Blitz.

A few months later, between January and April 1944, came the so-called Baby Blitz. This involved heavier raids than London had experienced since May 1941, although not on the scale of the Blitz itself (2.62 to 2.64). The last significant raid in this phase occurred on 18 April 1944. Again, attacks by manned aircraft became few and far between after this. The last serious attack of the war by manned aircraft came on 3 March 1945.

The final phase of London's ordeal started in mid-1944. This time it had to face unmanned aircraft attacks.

2.64. Plaque inside St Dunstan, in the West Church, Fleet Street, EC4.

THE TOWER, John Shaw's masterpiece (1832), heavily damaged by enemy action on 24th March 1944, was restored by Viscount Camrose in January 1950.

THE ALTAR and CLERESTORY WINDOWS damaged by enemy action between September 1940 and March 1944 were restored from the designs of Gerald E.R. Smith of the Nicholson Stained Glass Studios in March 1950.

Chapter 3

V for Revenge:
The V Weapons

It was 13 June 1944, and perhaps for the first time in WW2 the population of Britain could start to feel quietly confident that the Allies could actually win the war. The awfulness of the London Blitz had come to an end just over three years earlier, the last significant raid of the Baby Blitz had taken place nearly two months earlier, and surely now the Germans had more pressing concerns than to resume bombing raids on London. For it was exactly one week after D-day, the long awaited massed Allied invasion into Normandy in France: the start of the liberation of continental Europe from German occupation and control. It was proving to be no walkover, but the Allies were advancing, with progress better than the pessimists might have forecast. Yes, the Luftwaffe really had its hands full now. So what can have caused that big explosion at the railway bridge in Grove Road in the East End this morning?

It turned out to be the first flying bomb of London's war (3.1). The *Vergeltungswaffe-Eins*, or V1, (Revenge or Vengeance weapon number 1, 3.2) had been developed by the Luftwaffe as an inexpensive weapon carrying a significant HE payload yet requiring no crew. The V1 (often referred to by the public as the 'doodlebug') was about 25 feet (8m) long, powered by a pulsejet engine, and launched (initially) from fixed ramps on launch sites in northern France. The

3.1. Plaque, Grove Road railway bridge, E3.

3.2. V1 on display in the Imperial War Museum, Lambeth Road, SE1.

direction and duration of flight were pre-set (although the accuracy was such that only a region of London, such as the central area, could be targeted: this was not pin-point 'smart' bombing). Their average speed was of the order 350mph, with a range of up to about 150 miles. They each carried about 900kg of HE, producing about the same amount of damage to property as the larger conventional HE bombs dropped from aircraft earlier in WW2.

Over 9,000 V1s were launched against England during the war, with London the main target, but fortunately many of these failed to successfully cross the English Channel. Once they were detected, air-raid sirens were sounded but because of the numbers arriving, raids might continue for days at a time, with people often losing track of whether or not the all clear signal had been given. Their propulsion system gave the V1 a peculiar sound whilst in flight (another of its nicknames was the 'buzz bomb'). However, once the pre-set distance had been reached, elevators at the rear of the flying bomb were activated, sending it into a dive. This caused the fuel supply to the engine to be cut off abruptly, and with it the sound of the engine. This had an apparently unintentional result: if you heard a V1 fly overhead, you knew you were safe, and that some other poor souls might be hit, but if you heard one approach and then heard the engine cut out, you needed to take cover…now! There would be about twelve seconds of terrifying silence before the bomb landed and exploded, and unless you could actually see it in the sky, you would have no real idea of where it would land. Taking cover in an air raid shelter or Underground station was seldom possible.

Londoners' ordeal was dreadful. The peak period of the V1 attacks (between 13 June and 1 September 1944) saw over 900 V1s land in the LCC&CA (see Appendix 4). This means that, on average, about 11.5 V1s landed in the area each day: about one every two hours for eighty-one consecutive days. After all, being a 'robot weapon' programmed before launch, they could be fired twenty-four hours a day, regardless of the weather or if the night was moonless, or if trained flying crew were available...

Not surprisingly, the damage caused by a V1 depended on where it landed. One estimate put the average damage to property in a built-up area at about twenty to thirty houses demolished beyond repair, with some damage to 400 or more others. Similarly, casualty figures depended on the site hit, and the time of day. As we shall see, some of the worst V weapon incidents, as far as casualties inflicted, occurred during the day in busy shopping areas and other places where many unlucky people were gathered together. Just as in the Blitz itself, the large HE explosion killed directly by blast injury, as well as from flying debris, collapse of buildings, and so on. Fortunately, V1s caused relatively few fires.

Once the advancing Allied forces in France had captured the fixed V1 launching sites in early September 1944, the number of V1s landing in the LCC&CA fell (but they did not stop until mid January 1945). At around this time the Luftwaffe started to launch V1s from airborne aircraft over the North Sea, so they continued to land, although less frequently than before. And then at about 6.45pm on Friday 8 September 1944, two loud 'explosions' in quick succession were heard coming from Staveley Road in Chiswick, a little less than one and a half miles west of the LCC&CA. What was the cause? There had long been talk of another German secret weapon to rival the V1. Was this it? The British government explained the damage, and the resulting dead and injured, as a gas main explosion. So long did they continue with this story, in the face of continuing such events in south east England, that people began to talk, with bitter humour, of 'flying gas mains'!

In fact it was a new weapon – the V2 (3.3).

This was a chilling weapon indeed. Although containing about the same amount of HE as a V1, and causing a broadly similar amount of damage and injury, it was larger (about 47 feet or 14m in length). It was a ballistic missile, the development of which had been started by the German army (not the Luftwaffe who developed the V1) during the 1930s in secret, despite (as a rocket) not being explicitly prohibited under the Versailles treaty. It was fired from mobile launchers in Holland from where London was just within its 200 or so mile range. It reached an altitude of about fifty to sixty miles before falling back faster than the speed of sound (the double 'explosions' it caused were the sound of the actual explosion of the rocket, followed by the sonic boom caused by its speed). Time from launch to impact was four to five minutes. It was no more accurate than the V1.

Whereas the V1 could be heard approaching, could be tracked by radar, could be brought down by anti-aircraft guns or RAF fighters, could come to grief in the wire cables mooring barrage balloons, and whose approach could be signalled by the air-raid siren, none of these applied to the V2. There was no warning. There was no defence.

The worst death toll in a V1 incident, put at about 121, came early on in the campaign when the Guards Chapel in Westminster

3.3. V2 on display in the Imperial War Museum, Lambeth Road, SE1. The size of the beast is evident in comparison with the people standing close to its base.

TO THE MEMORY OF
THOSE WHO DIED
IN THE GUARDS CHAPEL
DESTROYED BY ENEMY ACTION
DURING MORNING SERVICE
SUNDAY 18TH JUNE 1944

3.4. A simple brass plaque by a window close to the inscription in 3.5, Guards Chapel, Birdcage Walk, SW1.

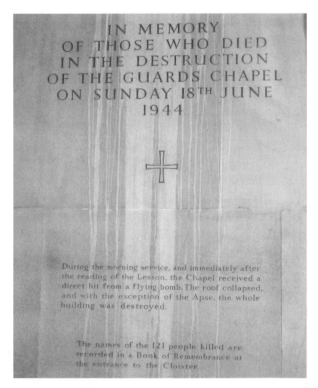

IN MEMORY
OF THOSE WHO DIED
IN THE DESTRUCTION
OF THE GUARDS CHAPEL
ON SUNDAY 18TH JUNE
1944

During the morning service, and immediately after
the reading of the Lesson, the Chapel received a
direct hit from a flying bomb. The roof collapsed,
and with the exception of the Apse, the whole
building was destroyed.

The names of the 121 people killed are
recorded in a Book of Remembrance at
the entrance to the Cloister.

3.5. 'During the morning service, and immediately after the reading of the Lesson, the Chapel received a direct hit from a flying bomb. The roof collapsed, and with the exception of the Apse, the whole building was destroyed'. Guards Chapel, Birdcage Walk, SW1.

received a direct hit during morning service on Sunday 18 June 1944 (3.4 and 3.5).

There was also heavy loss of life in Chelsea on 3 July 1944 (3.6 and 3.7). A Canadian firefighter was killed on the same date in a separate incident at Putney Heath (3.8).

The Church of the Royal Artillery Barracks in Woolwich was badly damaged on 13 July 1944, fortunately not during a service (3.9; see also 5.20). Similarly, two weeks later, on 27 July, Streatham High School for Girls was hit, but at night (3.10). However, there was heavy loss of life the next day when a V1 hit the busy street market in Lewisham town centre at about 9.40am on Friday 28 July 1944 (3.11).

IN MEMORY OF
THE 74 AMERICAN MILITARY PERSONNEL
OF THE UNITED STATES ARMY
AND THREE CIVILIANS
WHO WERE KILLED ON THE 3RD JULY 1944
BY A 'VI' FLYING BOMB
IN SLOANE COURT EAST / TURKS ROW

WE WILL REMEMBER THEM

3.6. Wall plaque,
Turks Row, SW3.

3.7. A metal plaque set into
the pavement on the
opposite side of the street to
the plaque in 3.6 is rather
vague about the same
incident.

IN MEMORY OF
ALMOST
100 AMERICAN GIs AND
WACs KILLED AT SLOANE
COURT BY A GERMAN
V-1 IN
1944

In Memory of
three members of
The Corps of (Civilian) Canadian Fire Fighters

Fireman J. S. Coull (Winnipeg)
who died as a result of enemy action
when a VI flying bomb fell on part of
Wildcroft Manor, adjacent to this site
on 3rd July 1944
also
Section Leader A. Lapierre (Montreal)
who died in a road accident in Bristol
on 30th April 1943
and
Section Leader L.E. ("Curly") Woodhead (Saskatoon)
who died while training in Hampshire
on 16th June 1944

The Corps of (Civilian) Canadian Fire Fighters
comprised 406 firefighters who volunteered to assist
the National Fire Service in the defence of Britain
between 1942 and 1944

These men were stationed in the four port cities of
Southampton, Portsmouth, Plymouth and Bristol
and their Headquarters were located at
10-14 Inner Park Road, Wimbledon.

© FR 2003

3.8. Plaque outside Telegraph
Arms, Telegraph Road, SW15.
The headquarters building in
Inner Park Road, Wimbledon,
no longer exists.

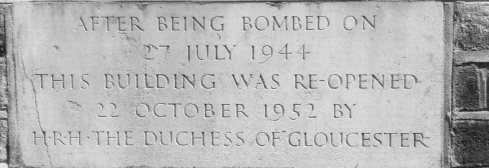

3.9. Plaque on wall of Royal Garrison Church, Grand Depot Road, SE18.

3.10. Plaque outside Streatham Hill High School for Girls, Daysbrook Road, SW2.

3.11. Plaque set into the pavement outside Marks & Spencer's store, Lewisham High Street, SE13. The inscription, which is extremely difficult to photograph, reads 'This plaque commemorates the fifty one people killed by a V1 flying bomb which landed on the market place in Lewisham High Street on the 28th July 1944'. I feel sure that few local people know it is there; perhaps it should be resited.

3.12. Inscription on a slab set into the ground just outside Chatsworth Baptist Church, Chatsworth Way, SE27, relates to the reopening of the church which replaced 'the church which was destroyed on this site on 18th September 1944'.

The first V2 to land in the LCC&CA came down in Woolwich on 14 September 1944. The third, four days later, destroyed the Baptist church in Chatsworth Way in Lambeth (3.12). Britain's worst death toll from a V2 incident came on Saturday 25 November 1944. The rocket landed at lunchtime, hitting a crowded Woolworth's store in Deptford. Officially, there were 160 fatalities. The real figure is anyone's guess (3.13). Five people died when the east wing of the Chelsea Hospital was hit by a V2 on 3 January 1945 (3.14). The same block had previously been badly damaged by bombing in WW1 (1.19), but had been rebuilt subsequently.

The largest death toll from any V weapon incident in the City of London occurred in the late morning of Thursday 8 March 1945 at Smithfield Market, Charterhouse Street, EC1. The story goes that the building in the north-west corner of the Central Markets complex at Smithfield was busy with shoppers because consignments of (non-rationed) fish and rabbits had come in. The V2 rocket apparently passed straight down through the building and exploded

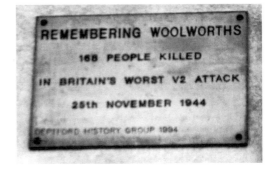

3.14. Wall plaque, east wing, Royal Hospital Chelsea, Royal Hospital Road, SW3. It reads, 'The main part of this North East Wing of the Royal Hospital was destroyed by a 500 lb bomb dropped by a German aircraft on the night of 16th February 1918 causing the loss of five lives. It was rebuilt in 1921 in its original form. The new building was again destroyed on the 3rd January 1945 by a German V2 rocket causing the loss of five lives and injury to nineteen other persons. It was again rebuilt in 1965 and was opened on 24th January 1966 by the Prime Minister'.

3.13. Wall plaque, New Cross Road, SE14.

REMEMBERING WOOLWORTHS

168 PEOPLE KILLED

IN BRITAIN'S WORST V2 ATTACK

25th NOVEMBER 1944

DEPTFORD HISTORY GROUP 1994

in the Underground railway underneath. At least 100 people died. The incident is noteworthy, at least in part, for being the last bomb of any kind to fall on the City in WW2 (the building was actually sited partly within the City and partly in the Borough of Finsbury).

A garden now marks the site of the Whitefield Memorial Tabernacle destroyed by a V2 on 25 March 1945 (3.15).

The last bomb of any kind to fall in the LCC&CA, and the second last V2 to land in Britain, in WW2 came down at Hughes Mansions in Stepney on 27 March 1945. Again, the death toll was heavy (3.16).

'Our Glass' 11. Out of the Ruins of War

CENTRE IMAGE: *'Bomb Site, Tottenham Court Road'*, Holborn Library Local Studies Centre, Wartime Camden. Whitefield Tabernacle was destroyed by a V2 rocket on Palm Sunday 1945.

EMERGING FROM THE BOMBSITE (above) *'Homecoming, 1945'* (Hulton Picture Library). Soldier returns to family, housed in one of the new 'prefabs'. MID LEFT: *Brendan Behan* (1923-64) first came to Fitzrovia as an IRA courier in 1939 but stayed on. His best known plays - 'Hostage' and 'Quare Fellow'– were directed by Joan Littlewood. The wags at the Fitzroy Tavern remarked: 'Dylan Thomas wrote under Milk Wood, Behan writes under Joan Littlewood'. *cont'd over*

3.15. One of several signs at Whitfield (sic) Gardens, Tottenham Court Road, W1. This one describes the V2 incident on 25 March 1945.

3.16. Plaque in gardens of Hughes Mansions, Vallance Road, E1. Curiously, Hughes Mansions are only about one and a quarter miles from the site in Grove Road in Bow (3.1) where landed the first V1 to hit the LCC&CA.

Chapter 4

Give Me Shelter

By the time of the Munich crisis in 1938, war between Britain and Germany seemed inevitable. Both the civilian population and its government fully expected Britain to be subject to air raids from the Luftwaffe. Such was obvious from history – both in WW1 and more recently in the Spanish Civil War the role of civilians in war was initially changed and then defined. Shelter from bombing was recognised as essential, but its exact form was subject to debate. The government feared a so-called 'deep shelter mentality' – individuals or families choosing to live for weeks or even months at a time in subterranean shelters in Underground stations or other deep shelters. They therefore resisted the use or construction of these.

At around the time of Munich, trench shelters in parks, commons and other open spaces were however begun. These were literally quite deep trenches, clad in wood, in which local people were expected to stand or sit during raids. Many cynics regarded them as little more than pre-prepared mass graves, given the scale of fatalities expected. As time went on, they became more sophisticated, with metal, brick and/or concrete sides and covers.

Also, before the outbreak of war, so-called Anderson shelters began to be distributed to civilians. They were largely constructed of corrugated metal, and designed to be partially buried in the ground and then covered with a layer of earth in people's back gardens. This was of course fine provided you had a garden; many (for example in the East End) did not. They were also of no value if a raid occurred while you were away from home, for example at work or at the shops.

To cater for those caught out under such circumstances, local councils constructed surface shelters, usually brick-built with a

4.1. The use of the crypt of St Martin-in-the-Fields Church, St Martin's Place, WC2, is commemorated by this stone. It reads, '1939-1941. The vaults and catacombs formerly containing human remains were reconstructed for temporary use as air raid shelters by the parochial church council of St Martin-in-the-Fields jointly with the City of Westminster...'

concrete roof, in the streets or on spare land. Other shelters were created in what were considered safe buildings – the basements of blocks of flats, warehouses, office buildings and department stores, and the crypts of some churches (4.1), as well as the basements of some private houses. Still others, sunk or semi-sunk into the ground, were sited in open spaces such as parks and cemeteries (4.2 to 4.4). Shelters were also constructed underground or half-sunk into the ground adjacent to council housing, for example, for local residents (4.5). Some were also constructed under railway arches, whilst some people merely took shelter under ordinary unmodified arches. Local authorities also sometimes built smaller brick shelters in people's backyards (4.6), especially those where it was difficult to erect an Anderson shelter.

It was only later, when people literally voted with their feet and occupied London Underground stations at night or during raids, that the authorities accepted their use and began to install facilities for shelterers, such as adequate toilets. In another climb–down, the government admitted (after the Blitz had been in progress for a

4.2. One of two semi-sunk air-raid shelters in Wandsworth Cemetery, Magdalen Road, SW18. Sheltering in a cemetery might seem macabre, but if bombs are falling, who cares? See also 4.3.

4.3. The second surviving shelter in Wandsworth Cemetery. See also 4.2.

4.4. The surviving outline of the entrance leading down to a sunken air raid shelter in the front lawn of the Geffreye Museum, Kingsland Road, E2. At the time, the garden was a rare green space in the Borough of Shoreditch.

4.6. This shelter was built in the backyard of 170 Stepney Green, E1. It is now occupied by sheep and goats at the Stepping Stones farm!

4.5. Sunken shelter adjacent to council housing in Bermondsey. Porlock Street, SE1.

while) that purpose-built deep shelters might fulfil a useful function, and their construction was authorised. Another large shelter existed at Borough Underground station – part of the original Northern line, a tunnel ran under the Thames to King William Street station near Monument in the City. Part of this tunnel was used as a shelter, providing accommodation for up to 14,000 people (4.7 and 4.8).

In time, there were many places for civilians to take shelter. Yet despite the impression which exists widely, only a minority actually took refuge in shelters of any sort during air raids, even in their own Anderson shelters. A good many people decided that they were going to at least try to sleep in their own beds, although many tried to reduce the risk of injury by bringing their beds down to the ground floor or cellar, or under the stairs, away from windows which when shattered by a blast could be lethal. Foolhardy? Not necessarily. Those who did go to a shelter were not necessarily safe from bombing. Unfortunately, for a time, many brick-built surface shelters were constructed using an incorrectly specified mortar mix. Some of these collapsed like a pack of cards when a bomb landed

Borough Tube Station

This was a station of the City and South London Railway that opened in 1890. The line was the world's first underground electric railway, London's first deep tunnel 'tube', and the first purpose-built railway tunnel under the Thames. In 1891 over 5 million passengers used the line. After reconstruction in 1922, the original entrance was relocated to its present corner site. During World War II a tube spur below was used as an air raid shelter for up to 14,000 persons.

HISTORIC SOUTHWARK

4.7. Plaque at Borough Underground station, Borough High Street, SE1.

4.8. A surviving entrance to the Borough station shelter (see 4.7).

nearby. Once this was remedied, however, surface brick shelters (as well as the Andersons) proved very successful in protecting against flying glass and debris from HE bombs, even those landing close by. Few if any could withstand a direct hit, but this was also true of some Underground stations, and other shelters in basements of large buildings.

As mentioned earlier, the government rather grudgingly agreed the construction of several deep level shelters during the early part of the Blitz, in October 1940. Eventually, eight were built. Those south of the river lie in a line along the A3, at Clapham South, Clapham Common, Clapham North and Stockwell Underground stations, while those north of the river are at Chancery Lane, Goodge Street, Camden Town and Belsize Park stations. The deep level shelters were long tunnels, each designed to accommodate about 8,000 people at a time. The designs were quite elaborate, with toilets, washing facilities, sophisticated sewage systems, etc. Each had two entrance buildings, one at each end, and most of these still survive (see Addendum to this chapter for a list of surviving entrances, and 4.9 to 4.15). They were completed in late 1942, too

4.9. Southern entrance building for Clapham South deep level shelter, Balham Hill, SW12.

4.10. Southern entrance for Clapham Common deep level shelter, Clapham Park Road, SW4.

4.11. Northern entrance for Clapham North deep level shelter, Clapham Road, SW9.

4.12. Northern entrance for Stockwell deep level shelter, junction of South Lambeth Road and Clapham Road, SW9. The decoration commemorates the fallen of WW1, and is relatively recent. The clock tower standing adjacent is older, being the Stockwell WW1 military memorial.

4.13. Warning at doorway to western entrance building for Goodge Street deep level shelter, Tottenham Court Road, W1. It is not clear if the writing dates from WW2, or is later.

4.14. Northern entrance building for Camden Town deep level shelter, Buck Street, NW1.

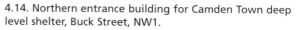

4.15. Southern entrance building for Belsize Park deep level shelter, Haverstock Hill, NW3.

late to provide shelter during the Blitz, but a few were opened to provide shelter during V1 raids later in the war. Other uses included billets for Allied soldiers. The Goodge Street shelter was used by General Eisenhower as his London headquarters (see Chapter 6).

Many structures were built to shelter the military and other workers. One ugly survivor is the Admiralty Citadel in Westminster, built in 1940–1 (4.16). Others were for the use of workers in Hackney (4.17) and Chelsea (4.18) town halls.

So, if you were out and about when the air-raid siren sounded, what did you do? You looked for signs for the nearest shelters. Some signs, close to main streets, directed people to shelters on side streets (4.19 and 4.20). Further signs were provided as you approached (4.21 to 4.24). Finally, there were signs at each individual shelter entrance (4.25 to 4.30).

With the possible exception of deep level shelters and the deepest Underground station shelters, no air-raid shelter could be regarded as completely safe. Sadly, there were many occurrences of multiple

4.16. Admiralty Citadel, Horse Guards Road, SW1, where staff working in the adjacent Admiralty building could take shelter during raids.

4.17 Surviving entrance to an underground shelter beneath the car park of Hackney Town Hall, Mare Street, E8.

4.18. Entrance to underground shelter in Chelsea Manor Gardens, SW3, immediately behind Chelsea Old Town Hall.

4.19. Large sign just off Deptford High Street, giving directions to the nearest shelter. Frankham Street, SE8.

4.20. Fading sign in Ladywell Road, SE13, visible from nearby Lewisham High Street, indicating the nearest shelter (see 4.21). Any direction arrow is no longer visible.

4.23. Sign indicating nearby cellar shelters, Carlisle Place, SW1.

4.21. Sign in Ladywell Road, SE13, adjacent to some steps down towards the shelter, which had a capacity of 700 persons.

4.22. Sign indicating nearby cellar shelters, Longmoore Street, SW1.

4.24. Sign indicating nearby cellar shelters, Lord North Street, SW1.

4.25. Sign for the Porlock Street shelter (see 4.5).

4.26. Shelter sign, Lockyer Street, Lockyer Estate, SE1. This is close to Porlock Street in Bermondsey (4.5 and 4.25). Note the different number on this sign.

4.27. Shelter sign, Purbrook Street, SE1.

4.28. Shelter sign, St John's Estate, Druid Street, SE1.

4.29. Shelter sign, Arnold Estate, Druid Street, SE1.

fatalities to shelterers due to direct hits or simple bad luck. Examples include: Camberwell Green shelter, 17 September 1940 (2.7 and 2.8); Coronation Avenue, Stoke Newington, 13 October 1940 (see Chapter 9); Bounds Green Station, 13 October 1940 (2.14); Balham Underground station, 14 October 1940 (2.16); Alice Owens School, Finsbury, 14 October 1940 (2.19); Kennington Park shelter, 15 October 1940 (2.21); Druid Street, Bermondsey, 25 October 1940

4.30. Shelter sign,
Longmoore Street,
SW1 (see 4.22).

(2.22); St Peter's Church, Walworth, 29 October 1940 (2.23); Stainer Street shelter, 17 February 1941 (2.36), and Walklings Bakery shelter, 17 April 1941 (2.48). There were also serious incidents at Sloane Square station in November 1940, Bank Underground station in January 1941, and at the Café de Paris, Coventry Street, W1, (which had even tempted fate by advertising itself as the safest restaurant in town, being situated underground) on 8 March 1941.

But the worst air-raid shelter disaster, indeed the worst civilian disaster in Britain during WW2, occurred at Bethnal Green Underground shelter at about 8.20pm on Wednesday 3 March 1943 (4.31). The story seems to be that the air-raid warning went off that evening, and people hurried to the shelter as usual (it was actually the first station along on the Central Line extension eastwards from Liverpool Street – but as yet unopened, its tunnels sheltered many East Enders during the war). The entrance was down concrete steps, with no central handrail and, in the blackout, very poorly lit. Nearby Victoria Park anti-aircraft battery was for the first time using a new type of gun, the unfamiliar noise from which was mistaken as the explosion of a new German weapon, of which there had been rumour for some time. Frightened, people surged forwards down the steps, a woman with a child stumbled and fell, the crowd pressed forwards... Over 170 adults and children died, crushed or

4.31. Plaque at entrance to Bethnal Green Underground station, junction of Cambridge Heath Road and Roman Road, E2. 'Site of the worst civilian disaster of the Second World War. In memory of 173 men, women and children who lost their lives on the evening of Wednesday 3rd March 1943 descending these steps to Bethnal Green Underground air raid shelter. Not forgotten'.

4.32. Gravestone in Tower Hamlets Cemetery, Southern Grove, E3. The inscription reads, 'In loving memory of our beloved daughter Agnes and granddaughter Ruby who were killed in the tube shelter tragedy on the night of 3rd March 1943'. There are other graves close by with the same date of death, but they give no hint of the cause.

suffocated, that night: a night on which, ironically, no bombs fell on the East End. Some of the victims were buried in Tower Hamlets Cemetery (4.32).

Addendum - Remaining Deep Level Shelter Entrances:

Clapham South: on Clapham Common at the junction of Clapham Common South Side, Nightingale Lane and The Avenue, SW4; and on the west side of Balham Hill opposite Gaskarth Road, SW12.

Clapham Common: behind hoardings on Clapham High Street at junction of Carpenters Place; and behind hoardings at junction of Clapham High Street and Clapham Park Road, SW4.

Clapham North: on the west side of Clapham Road beside Russell Pickering House; and in the yard behind Clapham North station between Clapham Road and Bedford Road (visible from Bedford Road), SW9.

Stockwell: on traffic island at junction of South Lambeth Road and Clapham Road, SW9; and behind garages in Studley Road (also visible from Clapham Road), SW4.

Chancery Lane: neither entrance has survived to public view.

Goodge Street: in Chenies Street at junction with North Crescent, WC1; and in Tottenham Court Road next to Whitfield Memorial Church and opposite Torrington Place, W1.

Camden Town: in Buck Street opposite Stucley Place; and at the end of Stanmore Place running alongside Marks & Spencer's car park from Underhill Street, NW1.

Belsize Park: visible from Aspern Grove; and junction of Haverstock Hill and Downside Crescent, NW3.

Chapter 5

Scars, Shells and Carbuncles

Vast numbers of buildings in London were damaged or destroyed in WW2. Many have disappeared completely, many more have been repaired, but not all the evidence has disappeared.

There are several monuments and buildings that still bear the superficial damage from 'flying debris', including shrapnel from exploding HE bombs, having escaped repair in the subsequent decades. Such damage at the Victoria & Albert Museum is commemorated with an inscription (5.1 to 5.3). Both the Tate Gallery (5.4) and St Clement Danes Church (5.5) show similar dramatic marks, as do the Ritz Hotel (5.6) and Holy Trinity Church in Clapham (5.7). The plinths of two statues standing almost

5.1. Superficial damage to the exterior of the Victoria and Albert Museum, Exhibition Road, SW7 (see also 5.2 and 5.3).

5.2. Superficial damage to the exterior of the Victoria and Albert Museum, Exhibition Road, SW7 (see also 5.1 and 5.3).

5.3. Inscription accompanying superficial damage to the exterior of the Victoria and Albert Museum, Exhibition Road, SW7 (see also 5.1 and 5.2).

THE DAMAGE TO THESE WALLS IS THE RESULT OF ENEMY BOMBING DURING THE BLITZ OF THE SECOND WORLD WAR 1939-1945 AND IS LEFT AS A MEMORIAL TO THE ENDURING VALUES OF THIS GREAT MUSEUM IN A TIME OF CONFLICT

5.4. Superficial damage to the exterior of the Tate Britain Gallery, Atterbury Street, SW1.

5.5. Superficial damage to the exterior of St Clement Danes Church, Strand, WC2.

5.6. Superficial damage to the Green Park face of the Ritz Hotel, Piccadilly, SW1.

5.7. Dramatic damage to an old memorial on the side of Holy Trinity Church, Clapham Common North Side, SW4.

opposite each other in Waterloo Place in St James's still show blast damage (5.8 and 5.9). Many other surviving examples of flying debris damage exist, including the Guards' Memorial, Horse Guards Road, SW1; buildings in Old Palace Yard, SW1; Westminster Abbey, SW1; St Paul's Cathedral, EC4; the White Tower at the Tower of London, EC3; and General Gordon's statue, Horse Guards Parade, SW1 (these are not illustrated). An unusual example of such damage is preserved near Lincoln's Inn Fields: damage to a plaque marking the site of the old head office of WH Smith & Son (5.10). Finally, there is surviving damage to the outer wall of St Bart's Hospital (5.11), which might have occurred in WW2, although at least one author ascribes it to the German raid in WW1 that revealed the old face of the gatehouse of St Bart's the Great Church (see 1.5). Examples of flying debris damage surviving from WW1 have been mentioned previously (see 1.6, 1.11, 1.14 and 1.17).

Sights such as these could be easily overlooked in the daily rush of life in the capital, but there are many sites in London that more or less obviously reveal some of the drama of WW2. The 'best'

5.8. Pockmarked plinth of the statue of King Edward VII, Waterloo Place, SW1 (see also 5.9).

5.9. Although the inscription appears to have been replaced since WW2, there is surviving damage to the plinth of Lord Clyde's statue, Waterloo Place, SW1 (see also 5.8).

5.11. WW1 or WW2? Damage to the outer wall of St Bartholomew's Hospital, West Smithfield, EC1.

5.10. An explanatory plaque explains the damage to an earlier plaque in Portugal Street, WC2.

5.12. Remains of blitzed buildings, Noble Street, EC2 (see also 5.13 and 5.14).

5.13. Remains of blitzed buildings, Barbican development just north of London Wall, EC2 (see also 5.12 and 5.14).

5.14. Remains of blitzed buildings, Barbican development north of London Wall, EC2 (see also 5.12 and 5.13).

5.15. Remains of a wall from a blitzed area, Cleary Gardens, Victoria Street, EC4. A small sign in the gardens records the story of the site.

surviving blitzed ruins are in or very close to the Barbican development (5.12 to 5.14). Another example in the City of London is a small garden sited in a badly bombed area, with the remains of a wall preserved (5.15).

Many churches suffered badly during bombing and V weapon raids in WW2. A large number have been repaired, but several have been only partially restored or have been left as monuments. The ruins of Christchurch Greyfriars and St Dunstan's in the East have been tidied up but otherwise left as they were (5.16 to 5.18). The tower and part of the front elevation of St Mary Newington Church survive alongside the replacement church building (5.19). The outer walls of the garrison church of the Royal Artillery Barracks in Woolwich, which was badly damaged by a V1 (see 3.9), still remain (5.20). Only the tower of St Augustine with St Faith Church, close to St Paul's Cathedral, survives: the rest of the badly damaged church has been completely demolished (5.21). St Alban Wood Street suffered a similar fate (5.22).

5.16. Ruins of Christchurch Greyfriars, Newgate Street, EC1.

5.17. Ruins of St Dunstan's in the East Church, St Dunstan's Hill, EC3 (see also 5.18).

5.18. Plaque outside the ruins of St Dunstan's in the East Church, St Dunstan's Hill, EC3 (see also 5.17).

THE CHURCH OF ST DUNSTAN IN THE EAST
STOOD ON THIS SITE FROM ANCIENT TIMES.

SIR CHRISTOPHER WREN REBUILT THE CHURCH
AFTER THE GREAT FIRE OF 1666 AND THE ONLY PART
OF HIS DESIGN WHICH SURVIVES IS THE TOWER.

THE REMAINDER OF THE CHURCH WAS REBUILT IN 1817
AND DESTROYED BY ENEMY ACTION IN 1941.

THIS GARDEN WAS CREATED BY THE CORPORATION OF LONDON
AND OPENED BY THE RT. HON. THE LORD MAYOR SIR PETER STUDD
ON 21st JUNE 1971.

5.19. St Mary Newington Church, Kennington Park Road, SE11. The patched up tower, and remains of the front entrance, survive from the badly damaged church building.

5.20. The remains of the Royal Garrison Church, Grand Depot Road, SE18.

5.21. The surviving tower of St Augustine with St Faith Church, St Paul's Churchyard, EC4.

5.22. The surviving tower of St Alban Wood Street Church, Wood Street, EC2.

5.23. Girdlers Hall in Basinghall Avenue, EC2, was destroyed in WW2. Part of the boundary wall has been preserved in the grounds of the rebuilt Hall. An inscription on the white stone just above ground level just to the right of centre of the photograph confirms its origins.

Fragments of other bombed structures also survive. One example is part of the wall surrounding the old Girdlers Hall in the City (5.23).

An oddity is the site of St Mary's Aldermanbury Church. The church was badly damaged in WW2. However, rather than being rebuilt in situ, it was dismantled, conveyed to the USA, and rebuilt

5.24. The remains of St Mary Aldermanbury Church, Aldermanbury, EC2.

5.25. The remains of St Alphage Church, London Wall, EC2 (see also 5.26).

5.26. Sign in St Alphage Garden, EC2, describing the history of the ruins of St Alphage Church (see 5.25).

St. ALPHAGE LONDON WALL

THESE RUINS ARE OF THE 14TH CENTURY TOWER OF THE CHAPEL OF THE PRIORY OF ELSING SPITAL WHICH WAS INCORPORATED INTO THE SECOND CHURCH OF St. ALPHAGE AT THE TIME OF THE REFORMATION. THE ORIGINAL 11TH CENTURY CHURCH WHICH WAS DEDICATED TO St. ALPHAGE, ARCHBISHOP OF CANTERBURY WHO WAS KILLED BY THE DANES IN 1012. LAY FURTHER TO THE NORTH AGAINST LONDON WALL. ITS RUINS WERE DEMOLISHED WHEN THE PRIORY CHAPEL WAS TAKEN OVER BY THE PARISH CHURCH. THESE REMAINS WERE EXPOSED WHEN THE SURROUNDING BUILDINGS WERE DESTROYED BY ENEMY ACTION IN 1940.

in Fulton, Missouri, in honour of Winston Churchill. However, the foundations remain in London (5.24)!

The remains of St Alphage Church, which had been incorporated into subsequent buildings on the site, were revealed by wartime bombing. They are now on display to public view (5.25). A notice to the rear of the remains from the main road reveals their history (5.26).

Many buildings damaged in WW2 were repaired in the post-war years, a time of austerity when money for such work was scarce. Some repairs are effectively invisible, others can be detected by the knowledgeable eye (see Chapter 9), while still others could at best be described as 'unsympathetic'. St Mary's Church in Bow was damaged during the Blitz. Despite it being built of stone (5.27), the tower was rebuilt in brick! The result is a strange visual incongruity (5.28).

5.27. St Mary's Church, Bow Road, E3, in the early twentieth century (see also 5.28).

5.28. St Mary's Church, Bow Road, E3, following the repair of wartime damage (see also 5.27).

Chapter 6

A Home from Home: Exile and Headquarters

If you are head of state, head of government or head of the armed forces of a European country which has been overrun by advancing German forces in WW2, where do you go? For many in this position, the answer was to take exile in London. Certainly, governments-in-exile of Norway, The Netherlands and Poland were set up in Britain's capital city.

There is a plaque to King Haakon VII of Norway in Palace Green in Kensington, W8, but as photography is not permitted in the area, this is a representation of the text of the English Heritage memorial there:

KING
HAAKON VII
1872-1957
led the
Norwegian
government in exile
here
1940-1945

The headquarters of the Norwegian government-in-exile was a short distance away (6.1). Queen Wilhelmina of The Netherlands took up residence in Belgravia (6.2). General Sikorski, Prime Minister-in-exile and Commander in Chief of the Polish armed forces had his headquarters in the Rubens Hotel, close to

6.1. Plaque, Prince's Gate, SW7.

6.2. Plaque, Chester Square, SW1.

6.3. Plaque, Buckingham Palace Road, SW1.

6.4. Statue,
Portland Place, W1.

6.5. Plaque, Frognal, NW3.

6.6. Plaque, Carlton Gardens, SW1 (see also 6.7). There is also a statue of de Gaulle nearby.

6.7. Plaque, Carlton Gardens, SW1, giving the text of a broadcast by de Gaulle to the French in June 1940, after the country had fallen to the advancing Germans (see also 6.6).

6.8. Plaque, Stafford Place, SW1.

THIS PLAQUE IS ERECTED
TO COMMEMORATE THE DEEDS OF
MEN AND WOMEN OF THE
FREE FRENCH FORCES
AND THEIR BRITISH COMRADES
WHO LEFT FROM THIS HOUSE
ON SPECIAL MISSIONS
TO ENEMY OCCUPIED FRANCE
AND TO HONOUR THOSE
WHO DID NOT RETURN.

CETTE PLAQUE COMMÉMORE LES
EXPLOITS DES HOMMES ET FEMMES
DES FORCES FRANÇAISES LIBRES
ET DE LEURS CAMARADES
BRITANNIQUES, PARTIS DE
CETTE MAISON
EN MISSIONS SPÉCIALES POUR
LA FRANCE OCCUPÉE PAR L'ENNEMI.
ELLE HONORE CEUX
QUI N'EN SONT PAS REVENUS.

1941 - 1944

THIS PLAQUE WAS UNVEILED BY
HER MAJESTY
QUEEN ELIZABETH
THE QUEEN MOTHER
ON THE 17 JUNE 1957

6.9. Plaque, Dorset Square, NW1.

Buckingham Palace (6.3). There is also a statue in his honour in Portland Place (6.4).

Other exiled military commanders include France's Charles de Gaulle. During his time in London during the war, he lived at several addresses including one in Hampstead (6.5). There are two plaques, in English and in French, commemorating his Headquarters of the Free French Forces in St James's (6.6 and 6.7), after the French government had surrendered to the Germans. In addition, there is an attractive memorial to the Free French Naval Forces, again near Buckingham Palace (6.8). Yet another plaque commemorating the Free French Forces exists in Marylebone (6.9).

There are also several memorials around London to the US commander General Dwight D Eisenhower, who was in charge of Allied forces for both Operation Torch in 1942 (for the liberation of

In This Building
Were Located The Headquarters
of
General of the Army
Dwight D. Eisenhower
Commander in Chief
Allied Force
June – November 1942
Supreme Commander
Allied Expeditionary Force
January – March 1944

6.10. Plaque, Grosvenor Square, W1.

6.11. Plaque, Norfolk House, St James's Square, SW1 (see also 6.12).

6.12. Plaque, Norfolk House, St James's Square, SW1 (see also 6.11).

6.13. The southern entrance building for the Goodge Street deep level shelter, Chenies Street, WC1 (see Chapter 4). Part of this shelter was used by Eisenhower as headquarters in the run up to the Allied invasion of Normandy in June 1944. The building has been redecorated and renamed in memory of this.

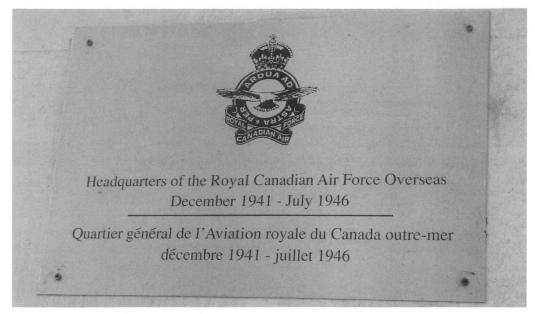

Headquarters of the Royal Canadian Air Force Overseas
December 1941 - July 1946

Quartier général de l'Aviation royale du Canada outre-mer
décembre 1941 - juillet 1946

6.14. Plaque, Lincoln's Inn Fields, WC2.

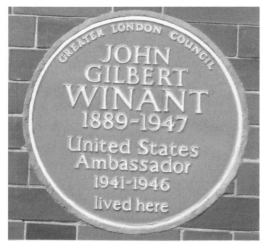

6.15. Plaque, Aldford Street, W1
(see also 6.16).

EDWARD R. MURROW
1908-1965
American Broadcaster
lived here
in flat No.5
1938-1946

6.17. Plaque, Weymouth House, Hallam
Street, W1.

6.16. Plaque, Winant
House, Simpson's Road,
E14 (see also 6.15).

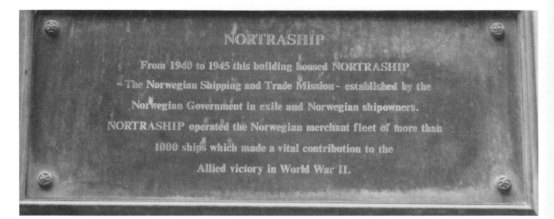

NORTRASHIP

From 1940 to 1945 this building housed NORTRASHIP
- The Norwegian Shipping and Trade Mission - established by the
Norwegian Government in exile and Norwegian shipowners.
NORTRASHIP operated the Norwegian merchant fleet of more than
1000 ships which made a vital contribution to the
Allied victory in World War II.

6.18. Plaque, Leadenhall Street, EC3. See also 6.1

North Africa) and Operation Overlord, the Normandy invasion on D-day on 6 June 1944 (for the Liberation of Northwest Europe). At various stages, he used offices in Grosvenor Square (6.10), St James's Square (6.11 and 6.12), and the very secure and bombproof Goodge Street deep level shelter (6.13).

The headquarters of the Royal Canadian Air Forces Overseas were housed in Lincoln's Inn Fields (6.14).

The wartime residence of the US Ambassador to London, J G Winant, is marked with a blue plaque (6.15). Harry S Truman, who took over as US President on the death of Franklin D Roosevelt in 1945, decided to replace him after the war: he later committed suicide. Winant is further commemorated in the East End (6.16). Another prominent American in London in WW2 was the then famous radio broadcaster Ed Murrow (6.17). His broadcasts contributed towards informing the US public of London's ordeal in the Blitz, in the time before the USA was drawn into the war.

The Norwegian merchant fleet was also run from London during the war (6.18).

Chapter 7

WW2 Civilian War Graves and Memorials

As in peacetime, the funeral arrangements for civilians killed by enemy action in WW2 were usually made by members of the family, with cemetery burials at an appropriate location (eg 2.24, 2.50 and 2.61). Problems of course arose, for example, if whole families were killed in a particular incident, if a victim had no traceable family, or if victims could not be identified (either because no one 'claimed' the body or reported the person missing, or if the remains were not identifiable). It is in situations like this that the boroughs themselves undertook the burials. Most if not all of the LCC boroughs had mass graves for these victims, where they could be buried. After the war, when the final death toll was known, almost all the boroughs erected a memorial at the site of the mass grave (for example, Fulham's memorial was unveiled in 1949, and Hammersmith's in 1953). Most memorials give a list of names: some boroughs only list those interred in the mass grave, others list those interred in the mass grave as well as elsewhere in the cemetery (eg 7.1), while yet others honour all of the borough's dead. Sadly, many memorials include a number of 'unknowns'. The borough of Finsbury decided to be different, as we shall see.

At the time I undertook the research for this book, there was apparently no single listing of the location of all these graves and memorials. However, after much effort I believe I have traced all that exist, and these are listed here (see also Appendix 3).

For convenience, these have been organized in order of the subsequent GLC boroughs, into which the Metropolitan Boroughs of the LCC were amalgamated (see Appendix 1).

7.1. Part of the Willesden memorial in Willesden New Cemetery, Franklyn Road, NW10. It states, 'The 76 names recorded on the adjoining screen wall are of those not buried privately and not otherwise commemorated'.

City of London (see Tower Hamlets)

Camden:

The Hampstead memorial is in Hampstead Cemetery (7.2), that of Holborn in Putney Vale Cemetery (7.3), and that of St Pancras in St Pancras & Islington Cemetery (7.4).

Greenwich:

The Greenwich memorial is in Greenwich Cemetery (7.5). The Woolwich memorials in Plumstead Cemetery are more elaborate: there is a 'general' memorial stone (7.6) together with a number of inscribed gravestones (7.7) on one side of the cemetery roadway, with another 'general' memorial and grave plot on the other side (7.8).

7.2. Hampstead memorial, Hampstead Cemetery, Fortune Green Road, NW6.

7.3. One of many civilian war memorials where the inscription is becoming difficult to read. Around the edge of the central panel is inscribed: 'Erected by the Holborn Borough council to the memory of those whose names are inscribed on this memorial and ten other persons unknown who lost their lives through enemy action in the Metropolitan Borough of Holborn during the world war 1939-1945'. The lettering at the bottom once read 'REST IN PEACE'. Putney Vale Cemetery, Stag Lane, SW15.

7.5. Greenwich memorial, Greenwich Cemetery, Well Hall Road, SE9.

7.6. Woolwich memorial, Plumstead Cemetery, Cemetery Road, SE2 (see also 7.7 and 7.8).

7.4. St Pancras memorial, St Pancras & Islington Cemetery, High Road East Finchley, N2.

7.7. Woolwich memorial (see also 7.6 and 7.8).

7.8. Woolwich memorial (see also 7.6 and 7.7).

7.10. Stoke Newington memorial, Abney Park Cemetery, Stamford Hill, N16. The lettering in the top panel is in very poor condition, and the whole memorial is sinking on one side and therefore tilted.

7.9. Hackney memorial, East London Cemetery, Grange Road, E13. The simple inscription is now becoming difficult to read, being indistinct with the lettering having 'bled' on the weathered brass panel. 'Metropolitan Borough of Hackney Air Raid Casualties'. The names of the individuals buried in the two adjacent graves are then listed.

7.11. Shoreditch memorial, New Southgate Cemetery, Brunswick Park Road, N11 (see also 7.12).

Hackney:
The Hackney memorial is in East London Cemetery (7.9), while the Stoke Newington memorial is in Abney Park Cemetery (7.10). The latter is unusual in that it lists those who died in specific incidents, including the Coronation Avenue shelter disaster (see Chapter 4). The Shoreditch memorial, sadly in a rather poor state of repair, is in New Southgate Cemetery (7.11). The text of the memorial is documented in the records of the borough of Shoreditch, held in the London Borough of Hackney archives:

1939-1945
Erected by the
Council of the Metropolitan Borough of Shoreditch

To the memory of those victims of enemy attacks on the borough
who are interred in this cemetery
May they rest in peace

'I am content to try to be worthy of the 1941 tradition of
Bermondsey, Shoreditch and the London Docks' – Mr. Menzies,
Prime Minister of Australia, in a speech at Melbourne on his
return from Britain, May 1941.

There are also two matching small memorial stones in St Leonard's ('Shoreditch') Churchyard (7.12). Judging by the text of the

7.12. One of two memorial stones in St Leonard's Churchyard, Shoreditch High Street, E1 (see also 7.11). They both read: 'Metropolitan Borough of Shoreditch Civilian War Dead 1939-1945. The names of the persons interred in this grave are recorded on the memorial erected in another part of this cemetery'.

inscription, it is possible that the stones in the churchyard have been moved from the cemetery, and indeed the Shoreditch memorial itself may have been 'rearranged' over the years.

Hammersmith & Fulham:
The Fulham memorial is in Fulham New Cemetery (7.13), while the Hammersmith memorial, unusual in being a horizontal slab, is in Hammersmith New Cemetery (7.14).

Islington:
The borough of Finsbury was unique in the LCC&CA in deciding not to have a conventional civilian memorial at all. After WW2, the council decided that a more fitting 'memorial' would be a sports field for use by the borough's residents! Even more unusually, the land which was purchased for the purpose was situated in Barnet (almost exactly ten miles away, which I would suggest with the benefit of hindsight is rather a long way to go for a game of football or bowls!) The whole of the memorial sports centre, including the pavilion, has

7.13. Fulham memorial, Fulham New Cemetery, Lower Richmond Road, Richmond, TW9. The central panel reads: 'To the memory of the 93 persons who here lie buried and of all other citizens of the Metropolitan Borough of Fulham who fell victims to enemy attack from the air during the World War 1939-45. We who survived dedicate this garden of Remembrance'.

7.14. Hammersmith New Cemetery, Lower Richmond Road, Richmond, TW9. 'Metropolitan Borough of Hammersmith World War II – Memorial to civilian war dead. During the years 1939-1945, 488 persons were killed by enemy action in the borough of Hammersmith. Of that number, 156 whose names are set out hereunder are buried in this communal grave.'

7.15. The abandoned Memorial Sports Centre and Pavilion, Stirling Corner, Barnet Road, Barnet, EN5, the Metropolitan Borough of Finsbury's original civilian war memorial (see also 7.16).

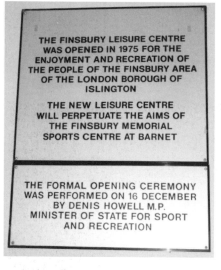

THE FINSBURY LEISURE CENTRE WAS OPENED IN 1975 FOR THE ENJOYMENT AND RECREATION OF THE PEOPLE OF THE FINSBURY AREA OF THE LONDON BOROUGH OF ISLINGTON

THE NEW LEISURE CENTRE WILL PERPETUATE THE AIMS OF THE FINSBURY MEMORIAL SPORTS CENTRE AT BARNET

THE FORMAL OPENING CEREMONY WAS PERFORMED ON 16 DECEMBER BY DENIS HOWELL M.P. MINISTER OF STATE FOR SPORT AND RECREATION

7.16. The surviving Borough of Finsbury civilian war memorial, such as it is. Finsbury Leisure Centre, Norman Street, EC1 (see also 7.15).

7.17. Islington memorial, St Pancras & Islington Cemetery, High Road East Finchley, N2.

long since been abandoned and, at the time of writing, lies desolate (7.15). A plaque in the entrance to the Finsbury Leisure Centre records the Finsbury Memorial Sports Centre (7.16), but is of course inadequate in that it does not state what the 'memorial' commemorates.

The staff in the Islington section of the St Pancras & Islington Cemetery assured me that the simple plaque close to the crematorium office was the memorial for the citizens of the Metropolitan Borough of Islington, although it does not actually state that (7.17).

Kensington & Chelsea:

Chelsea has not one but two civilian war memorials, very similar in design, in Putney Vale Cemetery (7.18) and in Morden Cemetery (7.19). The Kensington memorial is in Kensington Cemetery, and takes the form of a small memorial garden, marked with a plaque (7.20).

7.18. Chelsea memorial, Putney Vale Cemetery, Stag Lane, SW15 (see also 7.19). 'This garden is dedicated to the memory of those who lost their lives in Chelsea through enemy action in the Second World War 1939-1945 and whose earthly remains were interred here'.

7.19. Chelsea memorial, Morden Cemetery, Lower Morden Lane, Morden, SM4. The basic difference between this and the other Chelsea memorial (7.18) is that the names inscribed are different.

7.20. Kensington memorial, Kensington Cemetery, Gunnersbury Avenue, W3.

7.21. Lambeth memorial, Lambeth Cemetery, Blackshaw Road, SW17.

7.22. Deptford memorial, Grove Park Cemetery, Marvels Lane, SE12.

7.23. Lewisham memorial, Hither Green Cemetery, Verdant Lane, SE6 (see also 7.24).

7.24. Lewisham memorial (see also 7.23).

Lambeth:

The memorial in Lambeth Cemetery is quite a grand affair (7.21). It is pleasing to note that the memorial has been carefully refurbished in recent years.

Lewisham:

The Deptford memorial is in Grove Park Cemetery (7.22). The Metropolitan Borough of Lewisham memorial is in the form of a garden in Hither Green Cemetery (7.23) marked with a plaque (7.24) at the base of a stone cross. The memorial to the Sandhurst Road School tragedy (2.60) forms part of the garden.

Southwark:

Plaques to the civilian dead of the boroughs of Bermondsey, Camberwell and Southwark have been installed outside what used to be Southwark Town Hall, which now houses Southwark's museum

7.25. Plaques, Walworth Road, SE17.

7.26. Bermondsey and Southwark memorials, Camberwell New Cemetery, Brenchley Gardens, SE23. The very considerable numbers of names of the dead of both boroughs carved into the central black panels cannot be made out on this photograph, but may be read on the actual memorial.

(7.25). The main civilian memorials and mass graves of the three old boroughs lie together in a complex in Camberwell New Cemetery. There are two large memorials listing the names of those killed (7.26 and 7.27), and close by are the mass graves (7.28 to 7.30), with a small additional inscription by the Camberwell grave (7.31).

7.27. Camberwell memorial, Camberwell New Cemetery, Brenchley Gardens, SE23. The same comments apply to the many names on this memorial as to those of Bermondsey and Southwark (see 7.26).

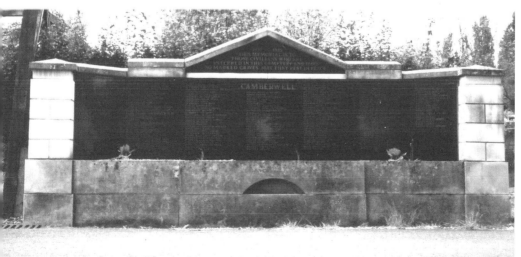

7.28. Bermondsey civilian war grave (see also 7.26).

7.31. Plaque by Camberwell civilian war grave (see also 7.29).

7.29. The words 'Borough of Camberwell Civilian War Grave' on this stone have become partially obscured with the years. The small plaque at the top is also shown in 7.31.

7.30. Southwark civilian war grave (see also 7.26).

7.32. Bethnal Green, City of London and Stepney memorials, City of London Cemetery, Aldersbrook Road, E12 (see also 7.33).

7.33. Central panel, Bethnal Green, City of London and Stepney memorials (see also 7.32).

IN THIS
GARDEN
OF REMEMBRANCE
REST THE BODIES OF 250
CIVILIAN MEN, WOMEN,
AND CHILDREN
OF THE CITY OF LONDON
AND OF THE METROPOLITAN
BOROUGHS OF
BETHNAL GREEN AND STEPNEY
WHO LOST THEIR LIVES IN
THE AIR RAIDS ON LONDON
DURING THE WAR—1939–1945

7.34. Poplar memorial, Tower Hamlets Cemetery, Southern Grove, E3. The bricks are said to be from blitzed houses in the borough (see also 7.35).

THIS GARDEN
COMMEMORATES THE LIVES OF
190 PEOPLE OF POPLAR
WHO WERE AMONG THOSE KILLED
IN AIR RAIDS IN THIS BOROUGH
DURING THE SECOND WORLD WAR OF
1939 - 1945
AND WHOSE MORTAL REMAINS
REST IN THIS PLACE

7.35. Central plaque, Poplar memorial (see also 7.34). All traces of the memorial garden that was originally laid out over the mass graves in front of the memorial were brutally removed by the GLC in the late 1960s just to make a roadway in the cemetery (see the back endpaper photograph in 'The East End at War' – details in Appendix 5).

Tower Hamlets & City of London:

There is a combined memorial/grave to the dead of Bethnal Green, the City of London and Stepney in the City of London Cemetery (7.32 and 7.33). The Poplar memorial is in Tower Hamlets Cemetery (7.34 and 7.35).

7.38. Wandsworth memorial, Wandsworth Cemetery, Magdalen Road, SW18. 'To the memory of those citizens of the Borough of Wandsworth who are laid to rest here having lost their lives through enemy action during the world war 1939-1945 and whose names are perpetuated on this memorial'. In fact, only four individuals are named. The 'twenty-four others unknown' could not be.

7.36. Battersea memorial, Morden Cemetery, Lower Morden Lane, Morden, SM4.

7.37. Wandsworth memorial, Putney Vale Cemetery, Stag Lane, SW15. The basic inscription is the same as that on the other Wandsworth memorial (see 7.38). However, this one lists just seven names and 'eighteen others unknown'.

7.39. Paddington memorial, Mill Hill Cemetery, Milespot Hill, NW7. 'To the memory of those who lost their lives in Paddington by enemy action during the second world war1939-1945 and who rest within this garden'.

7.40. St Marylebone memorial, St Marylebone Cemetery, East End Road, N2. The inscription, similar in form to that of so many other borough memorials, together with the list of names, is becoming quite difficult to read.

7.41. Westminster memorial, City of Westminster Cemetery, Uxbridge Road, W7 (see also 7.42).

7.42. Detail, Westminster memorial (see also 7.41).

Wandsworth:
The Battersea memorial is in Morden Cemetery (7.36). Wandsworth is another unusual borough which has two civilian memorials/graves. One is in Putney Vale Cemetery (7.37), while the other, mainly commemorating unidentified victims, is in Wandsworth Cemetery (7.38)

Westminster:
The Paddington memorial is in Mill Hill Cemetery (7.39), that of St Marylebone is in St Marylebone Cemetery (7.40), while the Westminster memorial is in the City of Westminster Cemetery (7.41 and 7.42).

Rest In Peace.

Chapter 8

Odds and Ends, Other Memorials and Fakes

T his chapter includes miscellaneous items that do not really fit comfortably into any other chapter.

Railings:

8.1. Vast numbers of metal railings were removed from around London in the early part of WW2, ostensibly so that they could be recycled into aircraft, etc. Traces of where they once stood can be found throughout London, this example being from Charles Square, N1.

8.2. As WW2 approached, plans were made to deal with what was expected to be a massive number of civilian dead and injured caused by air raids. All-metal stretchers were manufactured for the Civil Defences to use to carry casualties. Because so many were made, by the end of the war large numbers of them were left over. One use for them in the post-war period was as replacement railings, particularly around council estates. Their numbers are dwindling as they rust and are themselves replaced. These survivors are in Atkins Road, SW12.

Emergency Services:

This is the text of the memorial inside St Paul's Cathedral, EC4, set into the floor close to the font:

+

REMEMBER
MEN AND WOMEN
OF SAINT PAULS WATCH
WHO BY THE GRACE OF GOD
SAVED THIS CATHEDRAL
FROM DESTRUCTION
IN WAR
1939–1945

8.3. Many members of the emergency services, including fire personnel, police officers, ARP workers, nurses, etc died whilst on duty during WW2 (see also elsewhere in this book). The national memorial to firefighters who died in WW2 stands within sight of St Paul's Cathedral, in Sermon Lane/Peter's Hill, EC4. It was later 'taken over' as a memorial to all fire fighters killed on duty, whether in wartime or not (see also 8.4).

8.4. Inscription on firefighters memorial, Sermon Lane/Peter's Hill, EC4 (see also 8.3).

8.5. Memorial to Fire Service Personnel in the lobby of the London Fire Brigade Headquarters, Albert Embankment, SE1. The rear wall shows St Paul's Cathedral surrounded by smoke and flames. The inscription reads 'In memory of the men and women of the fire services of the London Civil Defence Region who gave their lives during the Second World War'. In front are bronze representations of three fire fighters in action. On the floor beneath is a diagram of the LCDR area (with the central district corresponding to the LCC&CA shown), and in front of that is a small plaque giving a brief outline of the history of the AFS and NFS. On either side are wooden panels listing the hundreds of Fire Service personnel who died. [For more information on the LCDR and London's Fire Services, see Appendix 1.]

8.6. Plaque in entrance to Eden House, Fulham High Street, SW6.

8.7. NFS plaque in Southwark Cathedral, SE1.

TO THE MEMORY OF
THE MEN AND WOMEN OF
No. 37 (LONDON) FIRE FORCE
WHO GAVE THEIR LIVES IN THE
SERVICE OF THEIR COUNTRY
DURING THE SECOND WORLD WAR
1939 - 1945.
THEIR NAME LIVETH FOR EVERMORE.

8.8. Two panels of the WW2 military memorial in the City of London Cemetery, Aldersbrook Road, E12, record the names of several members of the emergency services who died in the war.

WARDEN C.G. ARNOLD
AIR RAID PRECAUTIONS   20.4.1941
WARDEN G.W. ARNOLD
AIR RAID PRECAUTIONS   16.11.1940
CONSTABLE A.W.E. BEAGLES
CITY OF LONDON POLICE   11.1.1941
FIREMAN W.T.J. BENNEY
AUXILIARY FIRE SERVICE   15.3.1941
WARDEN MARGARET BRAITHWAITE
AIR RAID PRECAUTIONS   15.1.1941
WARDEN DORIS L. COLLINS
AIR RAID PRECAUTIONS   20.1.1941
WARDEN R.L. COLLINS
AIR RAID PRECAUTIONS   20.1.1941

WARDEN G.T. HILLS
AIR RAID PRECAUTIONS   20.5.1941
WARDEN F.B.S. KEMP
AIR RAID PRECAUTIONS   21.3.1941
WARDEN C.G. LE SAGE
AIR RAID PRECAUTIONS   25.1.1941
FIREMAN J.W. LEWIS
AUXILIARY FIRE SERVICE   11.1.1941
FIREMAN W.T. RASHBROOK
AUXILIARY FIRE SERVICE   20.1.1941
CONSTABLE A.G. RIDLEY
CITY OF LONDON POLICE   8.5.1941
STRETCHER BEARER D.E. WARREN
AIR RAID PRECAUTIONS   16.11.1940

8.9. One of two panels on the military memorial in Lambeth Cemetery, Blackshaw Road, SW17, listing the names of ARP, Civil Defence and AFS personnel who died in action in WW2.

STRETCHER BEARER W.J. OLIFENT
AIR RAID PRECAUTIONS
MESSENGER A.F. PLATER
AIR RAID PRECAUTIONS
WARDEN W.J. ROUTEN
AIR RAID PRECAUTIONS
WARDEN C.W. SMITH
AIR RAID PRECAUTIONS
FIRE WATCHER H. SMITH
CIVIL DEFENCE
FIREMAN W.J. SPENCE
AUXILIARY FIRE SERVICE
STRETCHER BEARER L.E. SPENZI
AIR RAID PRECAUTIONS
FIREMAN E.N. WILLIAMS
AUXILIARY FIRE SERVICE
FIREMAN C.S. YEELAND
AUXILIARY FIRE SERVICE

CORPORAL P. WELSH
ROYAL ARMY SERVICE CORPS

8.10. Grand memorial to those of the merchant navy and fishing fleets of Britain who died in WW1. Tower Hill, EC3.

8.11. Memorial to those of the merchant navy and fishing fleets of Britain who died in WW2. Tower Hill, EC3.

Other Memorials:

8.12. This memorial plaque at Dovehouse Green, King's Road, SW3, is more in the public view than the two Metropolitan Borough of Chelsea mass graves civilian war memorials that exist in cemeteries (see Chapter 7). The smaller plaque beneath is shown in 2.63.

8.13. A simple plaque on a bench by the bowling green, King George's Park, SW18. The actual bench has changed, but the plaque and location remain the same.

8.14. Memorial in Bermondsey. West Lane, SE16.

THIS MEMORIAL WAS ERECTED BY PUBLIC SUBSCRIPTION IN BETHNAL GREEN TO COMMEMORATE THE MEN, WOMEN AND CHILDREN OF THE BOROUGH WHO LOST THEIR LIVES IN THE GREAT WAR 1914–1918 AND WORLD WAR II 1939–1945, AND THEREAFTER ON ACTIVE SERVICE.

"THEY SHALL GROW NOT OLD, AS WE THAT ARE LEFT GROW OLD: AGE SHALL NOT WEARY THEM, NOR THE YEARS CONDEMN. AT THE GOING DOWN OF THE SUN AND IN THE MORNING WE WILL REMEMBER THEM."

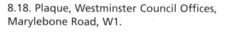

A memorial to the
Central Telegraph Office female staff
who helped keep communications
open during two world wars

8.15. Effectively, this memorial outside Bethnal Green Library, Cambridge Heath Road, E2, is both civilian and military.

8.16. Plaque, Postman's Park, off King Edward Street, EC1.

8.17. Plaque, Westminster City Hall, Victoria Street, SW1.

8.18. Plaque, Westminster Council Offices, Marylebone Road, W1.

WESTMINSTER CITY COUNCIL

IN RECOGNITION OF WESTMINSTER'S COUNCILLORS AND OFFICERS AND THE CIVIL AND EMERGENCY SERVICES FOR THEIR ACTIONS DURING WORLD WAR II (1939 – 1945)

THIS PLAQUE WAS UNVEILED BY THE LORD MAYOR OF WESTMINSTER CITY COUNCIL COUNCILLOR ANGELA HOOPER CBE FOR THE 50TH ANNIVERSARY OF VE DAY 8TH MAY 1995

WESTMINSTER CITY COUNCIL

IN RECOGNITION OF THE STEADFAST ENDURANCE OF THE PEOPLE OF WESTMINSTER DURING WORLD WAR II (1939 – 1945)

THIS PLAQUE WAS UNVEILED BY THE LORD MAYOR OF WESTMINSTER CITY COUNCIL COUNCILLOR ALAN BRADLEY FOR THE 50TH ANNIVERSARY OF VJ DAY 16TH AUGUST 1995

"FOR THOSE WHO LOST THEIR LIVES IN THE SECOND WORLD WAR"

8.19. Simple memorial tablet, Camberwell Green, SE5 It is situated close to memorial plaques to an air-raid shelter disaster in 1940 (see 2.7 and 2.8).

8.20. The WW1 military memorial in Grand Avenue, Smithfield, EC1, was added to in 2005 with a plaque dedicated 'In memory of all men, women and children who lost their lives in conflict since the Great War'. Apparently, the plaque is intended to commemorate local people, including those who perished in the V2 tragedy in March 1945 (see Chapter 3).

More Damaged Buildings:

The church was damaged by enemy action in 1940 and 1941 The work of restoration was completed in 1963 and on the third day of October of that year the church was rehallowed by the Lord Bishop of London in the presence of Her Royal Highness the Princess Alice Countess of Athlone

Maurice Foxell RECTOR
Churchwardens
W. D. Pryke · Douglas Copp · Ernest Mander
Ralph Lane · Ronald Copp

Architects
Alexander Gale
David Lockhart Smith

Builders
Duncan Cameron
Norman and Burt

8.21. Plaque, St James Garlickhythe Church, Skinners Lane, EC4, recording that the building was damaged more than once in WW2.

THIS HALL WAS REBUILT 1668 – 1674 AFTER THE GREAT FIRE
DAMAGED IN WORLD WAR 1914 – 1919
SEVERELY DAMAGED IN WORLD WAR 1939 – 1945
IT WAS FULLY RESTORED IN 1950

8.22. Plaque, Innholders Hall, Little College Lane, EC4, recording that the building was damaged in both World Wars.

8.23. Plaque on wall outside St James's Church, Piccadilly, SW1. It reads: 'The garden on this bomb damaged site was given by Viscount Southwood to commemorate the courage and fortitude of the people of London in the Second World War 1939-1945'.

THE CLOCK IN THE TOWER ABOVE WAS REPAIRED
AND RENOVATED AFTER DAMAGE BY ENEMY ACTION
BY MEMBERS AND FRIENDS OF ST MARY'S SPORTS
AND SOCIAL CLUB IN MEMORY OF THE FOLLOWING
MEMBERS OF THE CHURCH AND CLUB WHO MADE
THE SUPREME SACRIFICE IN DEFENCE OF FREEDOM
DURING THE WORLD WAR 1939 - 1945

JOHN BENSTED   STUART TREVOR HOLLICK
ALAN HARVEY CLAYTON   LINTON HENRY NIGHTINGALE
PHILLIP HENRY FRICKER FRANCIS WILLIAM ROBINSON
GEOFFREY GILKES   CLEMENT ALLAN WOOD

'AT THE GOING DOWN OF THE SUN AND IN THE MORNING
WE WILL REMEMBER THEM'.

8.24. Plaque outside the Church of St Mary and St John the Divine, Balham High Road, SW12.

8.25. Stained glass window, St Dunstan & All Saints Church, Stepney High Street, E1, depicting the widespread destruction of housing that Stepney suffered in WW2, as a background to the figure of Christ.

8.26. All that remains of the Mazawattee Tea Warehouse, Byward Street, EC3. This building was badly damaged in WW2 (see 8.27), but apparently little mourned as it was apparently a rather ugly building!

8.27. Plaque laid into the floor of the arcade beneath the old Mazawattee Tea Warehouse, which was 'demolished during World War II' (see 8.26).

Who goes there?

8.28. Pillboxes were small defensive structures sited at strategic points and manned by a small number of troops or members of the Home Guard in case of German invasion. This one survives at Putney Bridge Station, Station Approach, SW6. It is best seen from the platforms or passing trains, but can also be seen from the surrounding streets.

8.29. Another surviving pillbox (see 8.28), this time accompanied by the concrete elements of anti-tank defences. This one defends the pathway along the top of the Northern Outflow Sewer in East London. The nearest road access is from Dace Road, E3.

Oddments:

8.30. During air raids in WW2, it was not uncommon for water mains to be badly damaged, thus restricting the water supply available to the fire service to fight fires. When the tide in the River Thames was high, water could be pumped ashore for use against fires, but on more than one occasion big raids and big fires coincided with low tides. Once the problem was appreciated, static water tanks were instituted. These could be brick-built or metal tanks situated in the streets or other open spaces, and filled with water for later use. Many buildings destroyed in the Blitz left a basement that could be waterproofed and then flooded and therefore similarly be used to store water (see 2.58). These Emergency Water Supply facilities were marked with a prominent EWS sign. Such a water source lies on the Albert Embankment, SE1, alongside the London Fire Brigade Headquarters building. It was a pre-existing small dock, known as the White Hart Dock, and indicated as such on pre-war street maps. This may be the last surviving EWS sign in London.

8.31. The boroughs instituted First Aid Posts for the treatment of casualties in air raids in WW2. The No. 2 First Aid Post for the Metropolitan Borough of Bethnal Green was in the Outpatient Hall of the Mildmay Mission Hospital. The newly built hall had been opened in the late 1930s. The painted signs on the brick wall can still be made out (despite the subsequent graffiti). Austin Street, E2.

8.32. Plaque, Rossendale Street, E5. It reads, 'London Borough of Hackney. Air Raid Precaution Centre and Civil Defence Centre for North Hackney. Built 1938'.

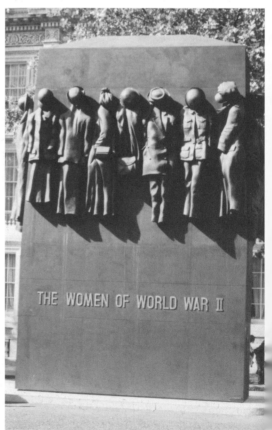

8.33. Memorial to the Women of World War II, Whitehall, SW1.

THIS PLAQUE WAS GIVEN BY THE ROYAL NAVY IN MEMORY OF

CAPTAIN RALPH DOUGLAS BINNEY CBE ROYAL NAVY

WHO, ON 8 DECEMBER 1944 DIED FROM INJURIES RECEIVED, WHEN BRAVELY
AND ALONE HE CONFRONTED VIOLENT MEN RAIDING A JEWELLER'S SHOP IN
THIS LANE AND STRUGGLED TO PREVENT THEIR ESCAPE. TO HONOUR THIS
COURAGEOUS ACT, CAPTAIN BINNEY'S FELLOW OFFICERS AND OTHER FRIENDS
FOUNDED THE BINNEY MEMORIAL AWARDS FOR CIVILIANS OF THE CITY AND
METROPOLITAN AREAS OF LONDON WHO, IN THE FACE OF GREAT DANGER AND
PERSONAL RISK, HAVE FOLLOWED CAPTAIN BINNEY'S EXAMPLE AND
STEADFASTLY UPHELD LAW AND ORDER.

UNVEILED BY

HRH THE DUKE OF EDINBURGH KG KT

ON THURSDAY 4 DECEMBER 1986

8.34. Although not strictly war related other than that the incident occurred in 1944, this plaque in Birchin Lane, EC3, indicates that violent crime still went on in wartime.

8.35. Plaque commemorating that many of Winston Churchill's morale-boosting speeches were made at Caxton Hall, Caxton Street, SW1.

8.36. Surviving painted camouflage, Stoke Newington Town Hall, Stoke Newington Church Street, N16 (see also 8.37).

8.37. Surviving painted camouflage, Stoke Newington Town Hall, Stoke Newington Church Street (see also 8.36).

Things Are Not Always What They Seem:

8.38. I had seen photographs of this sign in a couple of books, and had excitedly tried to track it down. When I enquired at the London Transport Museum in Covent Garden, their experts confidently identified the lettering as not being authentic London Transport or London Underground style. It is in fact an advertising sign in Tooley Street, SE1!

8.39. St Mary's Church in Whitechapel Road, E1, was badly damaged in WW2, and was demolished after the war. Altab Ali Park now occupies the grounds of the church and its churchyard. There is a layout of paving stones in the park that superficially resembles the outline of a church, but this does not correspond with the position of the church building itself (which is clearly shown on old Ordnance Survey maps of the area).

Chapter 9

Be Your Own Blitz Detective ('BYOBD')

If you live or work in London, why not consider spending the odd lunchtime or Sunday afternoon strolling around your 'local patch' trying to spot signs of war damage? In any case, you will probably see much else of interest that you had never spotted before in your rush.

The bombing and V weapon campaigns of WW2 changed the face of the Greater London area irretrievably. Large areas, particularly of the east London boroughs and the City, were devastated, but less badly affected areas were changed to some degree. Brick-built buildings were liable to collapse as a result of a HE bomb going off nearby, and burnt out or less severely damaged ones might be demolished rather than repaired. Even evidence of repairs may still be identifiable. So wherever you are in the London area, the eagle-eyed can spot the scars of war, especially with practise.

Many obvious examples of surviving damaged buildings are shown elsewhere in this book. So here let us look at some of the less obvious signs of war damage.

If a block of buildings or a warehouse, for example, were destroyed, once the site was tidied up the result would usually be a large flat open space, often cleared down to basement level. In the post-war period, large flat open spaces have been in demand for car parks and petrol stations, for example. While over time these sites disappear as they are developed and built over, some survive (9.1). The usual giveaway is the appearance along the edges (9.2). Smaller sites, often once part of a terrace of shops or houses, also survive

9.1. A bomb site in Shoreditch, now a car park. Tabernacle Street/Leonard Street, EC2 (see also 9.2).

9.2. The edge of the car park shown in 9.1. What remains at basement level may still be seen.

9.3. A bomb site at the corner of Upper Street and Barnsbury Street, N1, which has been turned into a garden. Note the sides of the adjacent buildings have been 'made good', and slight irregularity of the brickwork edge at the front at the junction with the building to the left.

dotted around, with some turned into small gardens (9.3). The now exposed walls of the buildings on either side of sites like these have generally been rendered in order to tidy up their appearance. When only part of a terrace was damaged, the edge of the first remaining building may show remnants of brickwork surviving (9.3, 9.4 and 9.5). The walls around advertising hoardings are another frequent site of surviving bomb-damaged masonry (9.6).

There are countless examples around London of terraces of shops or houses that received bomb damage, but where the gap resulting from clearance work has been filled in with more modern

9.4. The edge of a demolished building made good where it meets a surviving property. Tollett Street, E1. In the background may be seen the rear of buildings in Argyle Road, showing another 'edge' of a demolished bombed-out building.

9.5. This end wall of a demolished building shows not only irregular brickwork both to the front and the rear edges, but also the remnants of fireplaces along the line of the surviving chimney-stacks. New Kings Road, SW6.

9.6. More remnants of blitzed buildings behind an advertising hoarding, Goodman's Yard/Mansell Street, E1.

(some would say anachronistic) constructions. A few examples are included here to demonstrate the type of feature one might find.

One of the unluckiest houses in the LCC&CA was in Palatine Road, Stoke Newington. According to *Hackney at War* by Jennifer Golden (see Appendix 5), No. 48, alone or with its immediate neighbours in the terrace, was hit no fewer than three times by HE bombs between 8 September and 16 October 1940. A small relatively modern block of flats now occupies the resulting space in the terrace of late Victorian or Edwardian houses (9.7). Similarly, three slightly smaller houses have been squeezed into a gap in a terrace in Balvernie Grove in Southfields (9.8 and 9.9). Another example may be found in a terrace of shops with flats above in Battersea (9.10).

However, some of the biggest such sites, not surprisingly, resulted from the largest German HE weapons, either the largest HE bombs (see Chapter 2) or V weapons. On the southern side of a road in Southfields are two relatively modern semi-detached houses set into a gap in a long row of Edwardian terraced housing (9.11). While it is easy to imagine that the space arose as a result of a wartime incident much like those mentioned above, the true extent of the

9.7. Palatine Road, N16. A fairly uniform row of terraced housing is interrupted about one third of the way along from the left of the photograph by a small block with a pitched roof, set back slightly compared with the rest of the terrace.

9.8. The end house in Balvernie Grove, SW18, survived after some repairs, but the next three houses along had to be rebuilt because their predecessors were badly damaged in the Blitz (see also 9.9).

9.9. The rear of the houses shown in 9.8, visible from Standen Road, SW18. The replacement houses do not extend back quite as far as the survivors on either side.

9.10. This terrace of buildings in Battersea Park Road, SW11, shows a more modern section about one third of the way along from the left, again replacing properties damaged in the Blitz.

9.11. Two houses in Smeaton Road, SW18, rebuilt after bomb damage to the terrace.

damage caused by a single HE bomb – which fell on 6 November 1940 – is amazing. Contemporary records now held in the London Borough of Wandsworth archives show that these two houses occupy the sites of four houses seriously damaged in the incident. Other seriously damaged houses on either side were subsequently repaired and so survive. However, the worst of the damage suffered actually occurred on the other side of the road, and in a small side road more or less opposite. No fewer than twenty-two houses in both roads were completely destroyed or damaged beyond repair, with a further seventeen in both streets seriously damaged but capable of repair. It goes without saying that many of the remainder of the houses in these two roads were slightly damaged. Post-war buildings now occupy the most badly damaged areas (9.12 and 9.13). The V weapons could also cause serious damage on this scale: a good example of the damage caused by a V1 is demonstrated by the current buildings near Clapham Junction (9.14 and 9.15). Another example is in Wandsworth Common West Side (9.16). Finally, the site of the New Cross V2 incident (see Chapter 3) has also been redeveloped (9.17).

9.12. The houses shown in 9.11 are just visible in the far distance of this photograph taken in Lainson Street, SW18. The buildings on the left of the street were survivors. However, the buildings on the right of the street beyond a few surviving terraced houses to the right of the photograph are all more modern replacements of badly damaged properties from this single incident.

9.13. A further view taken in Smeaton Road, SW18, a little way down to the left from the buildings shown in 9.11. The tall modern block extends up the road from the junction with Lainson Street (see 9.12), replacing destroyed and badly damaged terraced houses, while the house on the near corner damaged in the same incident also needed to be rebuilt.

9.14. Junction of Elspeth Road and Lavender Hill, SW11, demonstrating the destructive power of a V1 flying bomb (see also 9.15). The whole of the end of the terrace of houses in Elspeth Road (and part of the terrace on Lavender Hill) was destroyed, and has been removed to allow slight realignment of the road and to allow a small garden to be provided.

9.15. Another view of the junction in Battersea also shown in 9.14. To the right of the photograph (between the central streetlight and the side of the building on Lavender Hill) is the garden shown previously. On the opposite (left) side of Elspeth Road is a modern block of flats built to replace the end of the corresponding other terrace of buildings destroyed in the same incident.

9.16. Another site of V1 flying bomb damage. This terrace in Wandsworth Common West Side, SW18, once stretched along much of this photograph. However, the section between the streetlight to the left of the photograph and the edge of the surviving portion to the right (marked by the tall wall bearing twelve chimney pots) had to be replaced by the modern block set back a little from the road, owing to the damage from a V1 explosion.

9.17. To the centre and right of this photograph of New Cross Road, SE14, are surviving shops with flats above. To the left, on either side of a small side road, are two blocks of buildings that replace those destroyed in the V2 disaster mentioned in Chapter 3 (see 3.13).

In all of these examples, some idea of the damage that could be wrought by wartime raids can be seen. It should be borne in mind that in the austere early post-war period in Britain, no more housing stock could be sacrificed than had already been lost, so as much damaged housing as possible was repaired. In other words, those buildings that have disappeared would have been irreparable, while surviving pre-war buildings immediately adjacent to these would have been less severely damaged, and so repaired if possible. It was generally a few years later that more wholesale redevelopment was undertaken, when more money could be spared for the purpose and the shortage of housing stock was not so desperate.

The cynic might well ask at this point how I know that all of these sites were caused by wartime damage, and not by, for example, peacetime damage or demolition. The answer to this is that they have been checked in the BYOBD's bible, *LCC Bomb Damage Maps 1939 – 1945*, published by the London Topographical Society (see Appendix 5). These maps, which cover the LCC&CA, show the information amassed during WW2 with regard to damage to the

9.18. Just to the left of the large tree more or less central in this photograph is a mock Tudor terrace that replaces a number of buildings destroyed in a bombing incident in WW1 mentioned in Chapter 1. Warrington Crescent, W9.

9.19. The section of the Peabody Buildings on the corner of Dufferin Street and Whitecross Street, EC1, was destroyed by bombing in the Blitz. Although the damaged section was rebuilt, as can readily be seen the brickwork in the replacement portion was not as ornate as in the surviving adjacent sections (see also 9.20 and 9.21).

9.21. (Left) The middle section of this residential block a short distance from the buildings shown in 9.19 and 9.20 was also very badly damaged in WW2. The repaired section can plainly be discerned against the adjacent surviving portions. Dufferin Street, EC1.

9.20. (Right) The rear of the buildings shown in 9.19. Again, although the style of the building including the windows and the doorway was maintained, decorative brickwork to match the undamaged sections was not used (see also 9.21).

9.22. Differences in the brickwork on this block in Tooley Street, SE1, can be seen, with the section just above the tree in the centre of the photograph constructed from bricks of a different colour to those of adjacent parts. This block was damaged on 29 December 1940 (see 2.31).

9.23. One half of the Old Hospital Block within the grounds of the Tower of London, EC3, was almost destroyed during WW2 by bombing. Can you decide which half of the building has been rebuilt and which is the original?

9.24. The rebuilt North Bastion of the Tower of London, EC3, following wartime damage. The main clue to which part has been rebuilt lies in the more modern windows inserted into the repaired section, compared with the cross slits in the original walls.

9.25. This block in Calvert Avenue, E2, lies adjacent to the main Boundary Street estate, built at the end of the nineteenth century. The left end of the block was badly damaged by a V1 flying bomb on 22 August1944. Although the damaged section has been repaired, the brickwork is not as ornate as the remainder of the building, and in particular the plain level finish of the uppermost floors is at variance with the more decorative central and right hand sections.

fabric of London's buildings. The damage is colour-coded, with black representing complete destruction at one end of the spectrum, to a yellow-orange for minor blast damage at the other. They do not pretend to be 100 per cent accurate (for example, damage to government or royal buildings is not shown), but are otherwise a remarkable resource. The dates of any damage are not recorded, but the maps do show the sites of all V1 and V2 incidents.

A further example of the results of the destructive power of aerial bombing may be seen in Maida Vale, a scar if you like of WW1 (9.18; see also Chapter 1).

The post-war austerity in Britain also meant that where repairs were made to damaged buildings, those repairs were sometimes made 'on the cheap', that is, to a lower standard or with slightly different materials than were originally used. We have already seen that the repairs to Bow Church were made with no attempt to match the surviving structure (5.28). Similarly, rebuilding of parts of the Peabody Buildings near the Barbican is still conspicuous owing to the materials used and the lack of any attempt to match the brickwork of the surviving parts of the buildings (9.19 to 9.21). The

9.26. Coronation Avenue buildings in Stoke Newington High Street, N16. At a casual glance, there is no evidence to suggest the serious damage that resulted from the impact of a bomb in mid-terrace (see also 9.27).

9.27. Detail from Coronation Buildings, N16 (see also 9.26). On the left, the section just above the window is original, and considerably more ornate, than the replacement section in the bombed portion to the right.

sites of such repairs may also be discerned elsewhere (9.22 to 9.25).

Sometimes, the clues are more subtle. The more one looks at British buildings, the more one realises that up until about WW2, buildings under construction tended to include decorative features, while after the war buildings became almost rigidly functional in their design. We have already seen some examples of how decorative features might be omitted when wartime damage was repaired. As mentioned in Chapter 4, an air-raid shelter disaster occurred at

9.28. The rebuilt Christ Church, Battersea Park Road, SW11, following severe damage by a V2 rocket.

9.29. The simple stone on the side of the rebuilt church (see 9.28) could have said so much more about the destruction in 1944 of the building formerly on the site.

Coronation Avenue dwellings in Stoke Newington on 13 October 1940. The basement of the block was used as a shelter but unfortunately on this date the building suffered a direct hit, the result being that five storeys of debris collapsed on the shelter resulting in many fatalities (as included on the Stoke Newington civilian war memorial, 7.10). The affected portion of the block was subsequently repaired, and at first glance the block shows no sign of the events (9.26). However, on closer inspection it may be seen that in the repaired portion of the building the arcuate structures above the windows are devoid of decoration, unlike those surviving from the original construction (9.27).

Vast numbers of buildings in the London area were destroyed or damaged in WW2. Churches are perhaps the buildings most likely to bear commemoration of wartime damage. Many examples are shown elsewhere in this book. One final low-key example may be seen at Christchurch & St Stephen's Church in Battersea. Christ Church in Battersea Park Road was badly damaged by a V2 rocket mid-morning on 21 November 1944, and subsequently demolished and later rebuilt (9.28). A simple inscription on a stone on an outside wall gives the barest of hints as to the violent and dramatic story behind the church's history (9.29).

I hope that this account has provided some idea of how an enquiring mind, backed up by some research in the appropriate Local History department, can provide an insight into the ways in which your local area was affected by war.

Appendix 3

London Metropolitan Borough WW2 Civilian War Memorials/Graves

Battersea
Morden Cemetery, Lower Morden Lane, Morden, SM4 (was Battersea New Cemetery)

Bermondsey
Camberwell New Cemetery, Brenchley Gardens, SE23

Bethnal Green
City of London Cemetery, Aldersbrook Road, E12

Camberwell
Camberwell New Cemetery, Brenchley Gardens, SE23

Chelsea
1. Putney Vale Cemetery, Stag Lane, SW15
2. Morden Cemetery, Lower Morden Lane, Morden, SM4 (was Battersea New Cemetery)

City of London
City of London Cemetery, Aldersbrook Road, E12

Deptford
Grove Park Cemetery, Marvels Lane, SE12

Fulham
Fulham New Cemetery, Lower Richmond Road, Richmond, TW9 (aka North Sheen Cemetery)

Greenwich
Greenwich Cemetery, Well Hall Road, SE9

Hackney
East London Cemetery, Grange Road, E13

Hammersmith
Hammersmith New Cemetery, Lower Richmond Road, Richmond, TW9 (aka Mortlake Cemetery)

Hampstead
Hampstead Cemetery, Fortune Green Road, NW6

Holborn
Putney Vale Cemetery, Stag Lane, SW15

Islington
St Pancras & Islington Cemetery (Islington section), High Road East Finchley, N2

Kensington
Kensington Cemetery, Gunnersbury Avenue, W3

Lambeth
Lambeth Cemetery, Blackshaw Road, SW17

Lewisham
Hither Green Cemetery, Verdant Lane, SE6

Paddington
Mill Hill Cemetery, Milespot Hill, NW7 (was Paddington Cemetery)

Poplar
Tower Hamlets Cemetery, Southern Grove, E3

St Marylebone
St Marylebone Cemetery, East End Road, N2

St Pancras
St Pancras & Islington Cemetery (St Pancras section), High Road East Finchley, N2

Shoreditch
New Southgate Cemetery, Brunswick Park Road, N11 (was Great Northern London Cemetery)

Southwark
Camberwell New Cemetery, Brenchley Gardens, SE23

Stepney
City of London Cemetery, Aldersbrook Road, E12

Stoke Newington
Abney Park Cemetery, Stamford Hill, N16

Wandsworth
1. Putney Vale Cemetery, Stag Lane, SW15
2. Wandsworth Cemetery, Magdalen Road, SW18

Westminster
City of Westminster Cemetery, Uxbridge Road, W7

Woolwich
Plumstead Cemetery, Cemetery Road, SE2

Finsbury
Memorial Sports Centre & Pavilion, Barnet Road, Barnet, EN5
(later) Finsbury Leisure Centre, Norman Street, EC1
Grave: Not known

Appendix 4

Selected Statistics

Accurate statistics regarding the bombing of London during WW2 have been perhaps more difficult to come by than might at first be thought.

Firstly, many published statistics relate to the LCDR as a whole rather than to individual boroughs or the LCC&CA, the area covered in this book. The latter area was fairly compact, extending from Wormwood Scrubs and Roehampton in the west to just beyond Plumstead in the east, and from Hampstead Heath and Stamford Hill in the north to Streatham and Sydenham in the south. The LCDR on the other hand was a huge area (see Appendix 1). Many published figures for numbers of bombs dropped on or civilian casualties suffered by London refer to the latter much larger area.

Secondly, casualty figures were in many cases difficult to assess even at the time. Some of those injured in a particular incident might be taken to hospital in other areas, and if they later died of their wounds they might not be included in published casualty figures. It is still widely believed that in some incidents not all the dead were removed from the site (see for example 2.21). Most harrowing of all is the fact that in many instances involving HE bombs and V weapons, the explosion would be so great as to effectively destroy all traces of some of the victims. There may also have been in certain instances attempts by local authorities to play down the 'official' casualty figures.

Finally, incidents occurring on the boundary between two neighbouring boroughs might give rise to inaccuracies in terms of numbers of incidents and casualties.

In short, all figures are subject to some degree of scepticism, which is why I have tended, in the body of this book, not to attempt to provide accurate figures for casualties in any given incident. Some statistics I have been able to obtain or modify from published sources I have included here for interest. Please note also that errors do occur in books, websites, and other sources (for example, it is not unknown for books to give the date of a V1 incident as having occurred much earlier in WW2 than it possibly could have).

Here, then, with the above provisos, are some figures to think about.

Table 1

Civilian War Deaths in City of London & LCC Area
1939-1945

Borough	1940	1941	1942	1943	1944	1945	Total
City of London	25	16	–	–	1	4	46
Battersea	196	81	1	19	165	19	481
Bermondsey	369	201	3	5	128	5	711
Bethnal Green	146	127	1	150	110	6	540
Camberwell	430	281	4	31	356	37	1,139

Borough	1940	1941	1942	1943	1944	1945	Total
Chelsea	184	77	2	–	98	12	373
Deptford	237	97	1	43	257	115	750
Finsbury	175	95	1	–	60	23	354
Fulham	285	23	1	17	224	2	552
Greenwich	192	116	–	7	145	26	486
Hackney	491	140	6	6	173	36	852
Hammersmith	229	35	2	3	173	31	473
Hampstead	105	49	–	2	67	6	229
Holborn	92	102	1	2	17	9	223
Islington	425	233	5	7	258	115	1,043
Kensington	239	63	–	2	136	2	442
Lambeth	681	417	9	8	355	63	1,533
Lewisham	437	214	5	90	362	43	1,151
Paddington	137	98	3	3	56	13	310
Poplar	293	251	–	9	85	17	655
St Marylebone	177	91	1	17	45	3	334
St Pancras	399	250	4	14	134	32	833
Shoreditch	278	182	4	3	41	25	533
Southwark	419	392	21	–	155	21	1,008
Stepney	367	270	3	18	117	143	918
Stoke Newington	107	22	1	1	44	5	180
Wandsworth	440	265	5	47	496	23	1,276
Westminster	226	316	2	2	110	2	658
Woolwich	192	157	3	11	199	43	605
TOTAL	7,973	4,661	89	517	4,567	881	18,688

[From 'Civilian War Deaths' table in *Statistical Abstract for London 1937-1946* (LCC). The table states, 'The figures include a very small number of deaths from injuries received during the 1914–1918 war']

These official figures are a little difficult to reconcile in some cases with figures obtained from other sources, relating to specific incidents. For example, the figures quoted for Chelsea and Westminster do not seem to take account of the known casualties in the Turks Row and Guards Chapel V1 incidents in 1944, but then of course many of the dead in both incidents were military and not civilian. However, also, just as a few deaths resulting from WW1 are included above, some fatalities would have occurred some time after the particular incident that caused them. However, they are 'official' figures for the LCC area, and clearly show the trends, including the dramatic dip in fatalities in 1942 and 1943 compared with the earlier Blitz and the later Baby Blitz and the V-weapon campaign.

Table 2

Density of V1 and V2 hits in the LCC area

Borough	Area (acres)	V1 hits	V2 hits
City of London	673	18	–
Battersea	2,163	34	2
Bermondsey	1,503	30	7
Bethnal Green	760	11	2
Camberwell	4,480	82	9
Chelsea	660	3	1
Deptford	1,564	30	9
Finsbury	587	5	3
Fulham	1,706	15	–
Greenwich	3,858	73	22
Hackney	3,287	38	10
Hammersmith	2,287	14	1
Hampstead	2,265	10	3
Holborn	406	4	1
Islington	3,092	15	8
Kensington	2,290	20	1
Lambeth	4,083	69	3
Lewisham	7,015	117	12
Paddington	1,357	5	
Poplar	2,331	37	9
Shoreditch	658	10	2
Southwark	1,132	14	3
St Marylebone	1,473	13	1
St Pancras	2,694	20	2
Stepney	1,766	30	8
Stoke Newington	864	7	2
Wandsworth	9,107	126	6
Westminster	2,503	31	2
Woolwich	8,282	82	33
TOTAL	74,846	963	164

[Modified from *London County Council Bomb Damage Maps*, London Topographical Society. Please note that in this era, imperial units were used and not metric: an acre is equivalent to 0.405 hectares]

Clearly, some of the difference in the number of hits comes down to the relative size of different boroughs, so if they had fallen entirely at random, the smallest boroughs such as Holborn, Finsbury, Shoreditch, Chelsea, Bethnal Green and Stoke Newington would be expected to receive far fewer than the largest boroughs (Wandsworth, Woolwich, Lewisham and Camberwell), which in terms of V1s were in fact the four worst affected boroughs. However, for a number of reasons, the hits did not come completely randomly. It seems that for the whole V-weapon campaign June 1944 to March 1945, the heaviest falls per unit area occurred, for V1s, in the City of London (most), followed by

Bermondsey, Greenwich, Camberwell, Lambeth and then Stepney. For V2s, the unluckiest borough was apparently Finsbury, then Deptford, Greenwich, Bermondsey and Stepney. [Again, these statistics are from the *Bomb Damage Maps* book.] Poor old Stepney and Bermondsey, which had both earlier suffered badly in the Blitz (see Table 3). In terms of pure numbers, Greenwich and Woolwich between them suffered about one-third of the total number of V2s to fall in the LCC&CA.

Table 3

Number of bombs per 1,000 acres (1939-1945)

>600	City of London, Holborn, Stepney
500–599	Bermondsey, Deptford, Southwark, Westminster
400–499	Bethnal Green, Chelsea, Finsbury, Shoreditch,
300–339	Camberwell, Lambeth, Poplar, St Marylebone, West Ham*
200–299	Battersea, East Ham*, Fulham, Greenwich, Hackney, Islington, Kensington, Lewisham, Paddington, Penge*, St Pancras, Stoke Newington, Woolwich

[* indicates the most badly affected non-LCC boroughs, for comparison]

In terms of weight rather than number of bombs per unit area, it seems that Holborn was the worst affected during the Blitz period September 1940 to June 1941, followed by Southwark, Westminster, Stepney, Lambeth, Finsbury and Bermondsey. I am not entirely sure how the size of a bomb could be estimated with any great degree of accuracy once it had exploded, but all figures in this table are again from the *Bomb Damage Maps*, London Topographical Society. In common with all the tables presented in this appendix, I have not attempted to verify independently the figures provided, nor have I checked the arithmetic.

Appendix 5

Selected Bibliography

Here **are** listed many of the books that I have consulted for this project, with a few comments provided for some.

WW1 – General:
The First World War. M Howard. (Oxford University Press, 2002)
[A concise account]

The First World War. H Strachan. (Simon & Schuster, 2003)
[Accompanied the superb Channel 4 documentary series]

WW1 – The Home Front:
All Quiet on the Home Front. R van Emden & S Humphries. (Headline Books, 2003)

The Home Front – Civilian Life in World War One. P Cooksey. (Tempus Publishing, 2006)

English Life in the First World War. C Martin (Wayland Publishers, 1974)

WW1 – German Air Raids:
The 'Baby Killers' – German Air Raids on Britain in the First World War. T Fegan. (Leo Cooper, 2002)
[Excellent concise account, with Gazetteer of raids on Britain]

They Come! They Come! The Air Raids on London During the 1914 – 1918 War. J Hook (published privately, 1987)
[A tremendous work, describing in great detail every raid on London. You may find it available from libraries or for consultation in Local History Departments. It was issued both as a single volume, and as a series of shortened accounts, each concentrating on one or two neighbouring boroughs. See also The Blitz - London]

The Inter-War Years:
The Origins of World War Two. R Parkinson. (Wayland Publishers, 1970)
[A concise account]

Britain and Germany Between The Wars. M Gilbert. (Longmans, 1964)
[Its 'approach encourages the student to deal in his own way with the problems raised by historical documents…']

WW2 – General:
The Second World War. A Farmer. (Hodder Headline Ltd, Teach Yourself Books, 2004)
[A concise account]

WW2 – Social History:
London 1945. M Waller. (John Murray, 2004)

[Excellent, concentrating on London throughout the war]
Wartime – Britain 1939 –1945. J Gardiner (Headline Books, 2004)
[It does exactly what it says on the tin]

The Blitz – General:
The Night Blitz 1940-1941. J Ray. (Cassell & Co, 1996)
[A surprisingly gripping account]

The Blitz Then and Now. W G Ramsey (editor). (Battle of Britain Prints International Ltd, 3 volumes, 1987, 1988 & 1990)
[An astonishing piece of work, really. This three-volume work covers the whole of Britain from 1939 to 1945 in detail. For my purposes I would have preferred less detail on individual Luftwaffe aircraft and their crews, and more on the effects of the bombing raids on individual sites, but a superb resource nonetheless]

The Blitz – London (including specific raids):
The Blitz. London Then and Now. J Neville. (Hodder & Stoughton, 1990)
[Not to be confused with the work listed above. Wartime photographs accompanied by more contemporary ones]

London At War 1939-1945. P Ziegler. (Sinclair-Stevenson, 1995)

London Before the Blitz. R Trench. (Weidenfeld & Nicolson, 1989)
[Each chapter takes a 'walk' around a section of the City of London, describing the buildings present before the war, and then finishes by indicating the damage inflicted on those buildings during the conflict]

The First Day of the Blitz. P Stansky. (Yale University Press, 2007)
[7th September 1940]

Blitz – The Story of 29th December 1940. M J Gaskin. (Faber & Faber, 2005)

The City Ablaze. The Second Great Fire of London 29th December 1940. D Johnson. (William Kimber & Co Ltd, 1980)

The Longest Night – Voices From the London Blitz. G Mortimer. (Weidenfeld & Nicolson, 2005)
[10th-11th May 1941]

The East End At War. R Taylor & C Lloyd. (Sutton Publishing, 2000)
[From the 1600s to WW2]

The Angel of Death Has Been Abroad. J Hook (published privately, 1997)
[By the same author as *They Come! They Come!* – see WW1 German Air Raids. In this series of works, the bombs falling on specific boroughs (and the resulting casualties) have been listed. Try libraries and Local History Departments]

The Blitz. C FitzGibbon. (MacDonalds, 1970; first edition 1957*)*

Hackney At War. J Golden. (Sutton Publishing, 1995)
[Includes details of every bomb that dropped on the boroughs of Hackney, Stoke Newington and Shoreditch in WW2, as far as surviving records allow]

The London County Council Bomb Damage Maps 1939-1945. A Saunders (editor). (London Topographical Society & London Metropolitan Archives, 2005)
[An immensely useful and interesting resource. Ordnance Survey maps covering the

LCC&CA with colour-coded damage records of individual buildings indicating the degree of damage suffered. The sites of V1 and V2 hits are also marked specifically. This will keep you occupied for hours and hours, but you will need a magnifying glass]

'Guidebooks':
London's War. S Van Young. (Ulysses Press, 2004)
[See next entry]

Walking the London Blitz. C Harris. (Leo Cooper, 2003)
[I found both this and the previous entry of interest, both describing walks around central London. However, both seemed, for me, to include an awful lot of subject matter not directly related to WW2. They also contain quite a lot of military matter]

V1s and V2s:
Flying Bomb. P G Cookley. (Robert Hale, 1979)
[Does contain a lot of technical information]

Doodlebugs and Rockets. R Ogley. (Froglets Publications, 1992)
[A good account]

Miscellaneous:
The East End Then and Now. W G Ramsey (editor). (Battle of Britain Prints International Ltd, 1997)

London's Secret Tubes. A Emmerson & T Beard. (Capital Transport Publishing, 2004)

Subterranean City – Beneath the Streets of London. A Clayton. (Historical Publications Ltd, 2000)

The London Encyclopaedia. B Weinreb, C Hibbert, J Keay & J Keay (editors). (Macmillan, third edition 2008)
[Another great reference book. Curiously, however, V1s and V2s are hardly mentioned]

Appendix 6

Some Places to Visit, and Contact Details

Readers are advised to check opening times and admission charges, etc, before setting out. Items on display may have been changed since this listing was compiled.

Imperial War Museum, Lambeth Road, London, SE1 6HZ. (020 7416 5320/5321, website www.iwm.org.uk). Free admission to museum, entry charge for exhibitions.
[An outstanding museum, that also puts on superb exhibitions. The WW1 and WW2 galleries are very good. Many German bombs, from both conflicts, are on display, including a parachute mine]

Museum of the Royal Hospital Chelsea, Royal Hospital Road, London, SW3 4SR. (020 7881 5200, website www.chelsea-pensioners.co.uk). Free admission.
[A small museum attached to Chelsea Hospital. Some interesting items]

Museum in Docklands, West India Quay, London, E14 4AL. (0870 444 3857, website www.museumindocklands.org.uk). Entry charge.
[An interesting museum, all about London's Docks and their history. It has a very good section on WW2, including a short film about 7 September 1940]

Churchill War Rooms, Clive Steps, King Charles Street, London, SW1A 2AQ. (020 7930 6961, website www.iwm.org.uk/churchill). Entry charge.
[The wartime cabinet war rooms, together with a museum about Sir Winston Churchill]

Museum of London, 150 London Wall, London, EC2Y 5HN. (0870 444 3852, website www.museumoflondon.co.uk). Free admission.
[I think the new WW1 and WW2 gallery is very disappointing]

Britain at War Experience, 64–66 Tooley Street, London, SE1 2TF. (020 7403 3171, website www.britainatwar.co.uk). Entry charge.
[A collection with displays about WW2, although entry is not cheap]

UK National Inventory of War Memorials, c/o Imperial War Museum, Lambeth Road, London, SE1 6HZ. (020 7207 9863/9851, website www.ukniwm.org.uk)
[The archive of the UK's war memorials, for all wars. Its database is available online]

Firemen Remembered (website www.firemenremembered.co.uk, contact: info@ firemenremembered.com)
['An independent charity devoted to recording and remembering firemen and firewomen who served and died in the London Region between 1939 and 1945']

War Memorials Trust, 2nd Floor, 42a Buckingham Palace Road, London, SW1W 0RE. (020 7834 0200, website www.warmemorials.org)
[A charity dedicated to the protection and conservation of the UK's 65,000+ war memorials]

Open House Weekend (website www.openhouse.org.uk)
[Held mid-September every year. Listings of buildings open to view may be picked up from local libraries in London from about the end of August, or from Open House London]

Index

* Westminster was awarded City status in 1900. However, so that the entries correspond with those of all other boroughs, and in order to distinguish the two phases, for the purposes of this index, I have referred to Westminster from 1900 to 1965 as the 'Metropolitan Borough', and from 1965 onwards as the 'London Borough'. I hope I have not offended anyone by so doing.